# SERVES YOU RIGHT!

To the staff at Viewmont... sure hope this helps to bring "service enthusiasm"... to your world!.

Susan Byrn

# SERVES YOU RIGHT!

### The Ins...the Outs...
### Great Customer Service

## by Susan Brooks

Published by
**Serves You Right! Ink**
Scottsdale, Arizona

To receive more information about Susan Brooks, visit online at www.servesyouright.net.

Brooks, Susan
    Serves You Right! The Ins...the Outs...Great Customer
    Service. No-nonsense lessons to heighten Service Enthusiasm®.
    A portion of book proceeds benefits the National Association
    of Women Business Owners (NAWBO) Scholarship Fund/Susan
    Brooks — 1st ed.
      p. cm.
    ISBN 0-9753018-0-2

2004092185
CIP

Edited and designed by The Speaker's Source.

# Dedication

*To all my "Serves You Right!®" readers
and clients who, in refusing
to settle for mediocrity, continue
to pursue their quest for
service enthusiasm and excellence.*

# Acknowledgements

To Kirk Nelson, who all but dared me to make this book happen and, thanks to his encouragement, here 'tis.

To Jim Fickess, my first editor, who believed in my ability and concept enough to publish my first few years of columns in Arizona's largest newspaper, the *Arizona Republic*.

To my stellar editor at the *Phoenix Business Journal*, Ilana Ruber, who continues to welcome my every column by agreeing to publish them "as is" without choosing to use her red pen.

To Joyce Thompson, my steadfast assistant, and Bob Henschen's team at The Speaker's Source, who, together and individually, translated my scrawl into a format that allows readers to discover their own pace and pleasure.

To my family and friends (you know who you are!) who have been my very own ever-present cheerleading squad, and . . .

To my husband and life partner, Barry, who is, and always has been, my greatest cheerleader of all!

# Contents

# Introduction

As a customer, can you remember the last time you had an over-the-top service experience? As a business-person, are you and your staff aligned to be Service Heroes for your customers? As an individual, can you remember making a difference by serving and reaching out to someone else? If these questions spark the least bit of interest (maybe even excitement), then read on.

As a young girl, I was inspired by my grandmother, who had a reputation as the matriarch in her field of interior design.

"Make your clients your friends," she told me. "A happy customer will bring you more happy customers."

When I birthed Cookies From Home with my husband and partner, Barry, more than 25 years ago, my dream as the visionary of our company was to make the world a better place by serving . . . no, treating . . . my customers to a "feel good" service experience while they munched on the best homemade cookies they had ever tasted. Today, Cookies From Home is a multimillion-dollar mail order and corporate gift company, and many of my happy customers year after year bring me more happy cookie lovers. And, yes, just like my grandmother told me, many clients have also become my friends.

Unfortunately, when I am the customer, I am often appalled by the mass of arrogance and apathy— demonstrated by a "whatever" kind of attitude—that I experience in the marketplace. Mediocrity has become the norm. I wonder if owners and managers know how their customers are being treated.

Having been in the trenches myself for so many years, I know what a mindful challenge it is to translate and transfer a vision of super service excellence on a daily basis. So I simply *had* to speak out. I *had* to do something about the "unconscious" attitude shown toward the NGE (not good enough) service that permeated my everyday inter-actions at restaurants, retail stores, medical offices, hotels, banks, and so on. I became a monomaniac on a mission to be the wake-up call that empowers others to give customers the service we deserve!

The *Arizona Republic*, as well as several other national publications, published my first three years of "Serves You Right!®" columns. The *Phoenix Business Journal* has been home to "Serves You Right!®" consistently since 1998. This book version of "Serves You Right!®" contains a collection of the most popular and controversial published columns, full of lessons and true-life experiences that I hope will stimulate thought, reflection and, yes, identification that propels people (maybe even you) into action as businesspeople and consumers.

Readers often ask me to identify the culprit companies I write about, perhaps for their own absolution. I deliberately leave them nameless so others might think I'm writing about them. However, I gladly sing my praises of the Service Heroes who do cross my path.

My greatest hope is that this collection of "Serves You Right!®" columns will inspire service enthusiasm. Giving and receiving super service excellence is what we all deserve. Service is the key, the competitive edge between good companies and great companies. Service motivates successful people to become champions. Service is how you and I can be that difference to make our world a better place. Service enthusiasm always, and absolutely, Serves You Right!

# Leading
# the Pack

# Starry, Starry Night

*Negotiating New Path*
*Requires Clear Vision*

Knowing how to grow your business, how to best serve your customer, how to stay in alignment with the integrity of your vision . . . these are the dilemmas that can keep a business owner awake all hours of the night.

It's been six years since I made the bittersweet decision to sell the lease on our retail cookie store and move our Victorian Parlor from historic Mill Avenue to our corporate/bakery facility just two miles away in a business park. I remember how heartfelt memories and emotional connections from 16 years on Mill clouded my mind when I first made the decision.

I remembered Barry, my husband and partner, building the store with his own two hands. I remembered Walt Richardson crooning his love tunes in our parlor almost every Valentine's Day. I remembered our then-young children asleep on sacks of flour while we baked our little hearts out through the midnight hour. I remembered so many of our college-age employees and customers, who are now all "growed up" with children of their own. I remembered my grandmother's wisdom and antique furnishings, which defined our company's image and philosophy.

When I looked out through the lattice and lace of my Mill Avenue storefront window, however, I saw Hooters and McDonald's. I knew in that screaming moment that the demographic shift for the entire area was already in process, and that's what prompted my final decision to move on. It was time to grow. It was time to let go. It was time to serve our customers in a new way. And, yes, it was time to step out onto those skinny branches once again and trust my entrepreneurial spirit and vision.

On this starry, starry night, while the rest of the world was sleeping, I sat wide-awake under a blanket of stars, knowing in that empty moment what I knew I had to do to grow my company. The next morning I called a meeting, first with Barry and then with my key managers.

We had been having lots of meetings during that time—talking, debating and arguing about "what to do with our store on Mill." We knew this move would stretch the loyalty of even our most regular cookie lovers. Casual Mill Avenue strollers who were used to following their noses into our turn-of-the-century parlor would now have to drive two miles down the road to our new location in a business park with frontage on one of the busiest streets in Tempe. Instead of being an over-the-counter retail cookie store, we were now going to become a Gift Center, which meant a considerable difference in purchase price points.

"Sometimes, as businesspeople, we stay with what has always worked simply because we've always done it that way."

SERVES YOU RIGHT!

Sometimes, as businesspeople, we stay with what has always worked simply because we've always done it that way. But most of us have learned that being in the groove of the familiar is only temporary. Times change. Customers' needs and desires change. Today we are especially challenged to think creatively about growth and service. What has worked in the past won't necessarily work today.

As the visionary leaders in our companies, it's up to us to find new ways of working and new ways of serving our customers while maintaining the integrity of who we are. Basic as they sound, the vital questions still apply: Who are our customers? Where are our customers? How can we best serve our customers?

If these and so many other questions and business issues crowd your mind, keeping you awake at night, surrender to an hour or two under the stars, where silence and serenity offer the greatest clarity for guidance and direction. Often in these early morning hours you can best quiet a busy mind and finally listen to the truth waiting there in your heart. And, read this book and join me on my own travels as I experience the business world from the customer-service perspective, learning some things "the hard way" or encountering unexpected flashes of insight.

# We must be the change
# we wish to see in the world.

GANDHI

# Be the Hero!

## *Confront Fear and Push It Aside*

Nothing moves quite as fast as fear.

Fear is contaminating and highly contagious.

Fear is paralyzing and unproductive.

Fear creates failure and loss.

Since September 11, 2001, we watch as our world unravels. Day by day, new implications and deeper ramifications of this horrific event make themselves known, from the global level right down to each of our individual lives. How will our world change? How and when will our economy fully recover? Will people still want and need the product or service we provide? How will we feed our children, pay our bills? How will we survive? These are confrontational issues and questions we are asking one another and ourselves because these are, after all, confrontational times.

It's up to us, as business professionals, to model our behavior after the Everyday Heroes in New York and Washington. In the face of ultimate danger and devastating despair, their intention of spirit and service ruled the land. Fear was confronted, then pushed aside as our Everyday Heroes committed themselves to doing "whatever it takes."

That's what *we* need to do, each and every one of us, as businesspeople and consumers: Confront the fear that grabs hold from down deep and push it aside so we can do "whatever it takes" to survive . . . and thrive.

In the aftermath of 9-11, giving blood, making donations and volunteering services helped, especially in the beginning. What we need to do now is spend money, make plans and move forward with our lives. Here are a few behavioral suggestions that worked then, and might renew your spirit and service enthusiasm when trouble strikes again:

**Declare yourself the CIO of your company: the Chief Inspirational Officer.** Set an example of confidence. Use positive language when you talk about the present and the future. Make decisions for and commitments to the future. *You* take charge; don't let fear decide for you. Inspire others with hope.

**Kindness counts . . . to your co-workers and to your customers.** "Lean and mean" management won't work in these times, and we are overdue in bringing the human spirit back to our balance sheet. Have you noticed gentler behavior in grocery stores and even on the highways? Humility and gratitude are very good things.

**Do "whatever it takes."** Stay mindful rather than becoming addicted to the struggle. Choose to be the hero instead of the victim. You know what you need to do . . . so do it . . . *now.* Stop waiting.

"What we need to do now is spend money, make plans and move forward with our lives."

We can do this. We are doing this. We *must* inspire those who are stuck. We must rescue our economy. Every day, every moment, we get to choose. Opportunity is all around us, just waiting to be found. Failure is not an option. After all, this is America, a country blessed with diversity and divine inspiration. You've said you want to help. You've said you want your life to make a difference. Here's your chance to *be* that difference by turning this nightmare back into the American dream.

# Service is the rent you pay for room on this earth.

SHIRLEY CHISHOLM

# Adults Only

*Leading by Example
Sets Bar for Employees*

Was it Ray Kroc, founder of McDonald's, who said he wanted to be in business *for* himself but not *by* himself? And wasn't it Herb Kelleher of Southwest Airlines who said his job was to take real good care of his employees who, in turn, would take real good care of his customers?

As leaders in our companies, our job, besides holding the vision, is to set an example for a desired work ethic and attitude for our employees, demonstrating dignity and respect at all times. We should be giving our staff the compassion and care we want them to give our customers and one another.

"Oops!" one business owner gasped at a leadership conference I attended recently. He confessed to frequent temper tantrums when life and its regular challenges interrupted his plans for the day. He had an excellent business sense regarding operations, process and profitability, but his people skills were tied to a short fuse.

Every day as I drive to my office, I promise myself I will stay in my Adult mode. I will keep a sense of calm, a sense of confidence no matter what. I remind myself that I am the leader of my pack, responsible for its well-being, protector and communicator extraordinaire. Then, when I arrive and walk toward my office, sunglasses and car keys still in hand, my assistant greets me in the hallway with a series of challenges that require my immediate attention . . . and it's not even 9 o'clock!

My first reaction is to remember to breathe. I quiet the Child in me, who wants to whine: "Can't you see I haven't even put down my briefcase yet? Why is this happening to me? I don't want to make decisions yet, at least not before I've had my second cup of coffee!"

Then my Parent pushes the Child aside, ready to threaten and punish whoever is to blame for these upsets, preaching the rightness and wrongness that should be clearly visible to everyone involved! Breathe. Breathe again.

Instead, I put down my sunglasses, car keys and briefcase. I symbolically put on my firefighter's hat and get ready to embrace the day. I attempt to solve problems by empowering my team while maintaining a positive "can do" attitude that helps my staff come to a solution no matter what the issue. At least, this is the behavior I do my best to exemplify most of the time . . .

As business leaders, we don't have the luxury of temper tantrums. In our companies, the outside reflects the inside. You and your staff breathe the same air. Know that whatever feelings, fears and frustrations you experience inside your head, the outside world will

"We should be giving our staff the compassion and care we want them to give our customers and one another."

mirror your reality. You, as the leader, are contagious! So to best serve your staff, which, in turn, best serves your customers, leave the Kid and the Parent in the parking lot. Keep your Adult ever present . . . and remember to breathe!

# Our greatness is determined by service.

D R .   M A R T I N   L U T H E R   K I N G

# Dream Messages

## Cynicism Fades when Shopping at Integrity

My husband had a dream. He always has dreams he can remember to share with me in the first moments of morning consciousness. This particular morning, however, he really got my attention when he said his dream was about a retail shopping experience. Knowing my husband would rather go to the dentist than go shopping, I was especially curious. Through osmosis, I guess (and perhaps because we've been married more than 35 years), my passion for shopping has somehow seeped into his subconscious.

He dreamed he was in a mall-like environment, and he was attracted to one small, almost closet-like shop called Integrity. Shelves were filled with unusual and attractive homemade merchandise. The ambiance was comfortable and soothing, encouraging the browser to stay awhile.

Sounded good to me . . . until he got to the finale: There was no staff . . . no staff at all. This was a self-help experience start to finish. That's right, even the cash register was unattended. People bought; people paid. That's why this was but a dream.

The honor system is a faded, hopeless concept of the long-ago past. In the real world, there's no way merchandise would not be stolen or destroyed. No way would a cash register have money left in the drawer. No way would people pay for what they bought, nothing more and nothing less. No way— except for a little soap store along the rural roads of Asheville, North Carolina.

We were visiting friends, soaking in the mountain air and experience, when my friend said she needed to make a quick stop to pick up some more herbal soaps and creams for her home. Off to the side of a fairly active country road stood a small, one-room shop a good distance away from the family home. A welcome sign by the front door explained that the owner was out of town for the weekend but invited us to go inside to browse and smell her herbal creations.

Fresh and dried flowers were strategically placed; hand-written attractive signage accompanied every product, explaining ingredients and the function of each; and, yes, there was an unlocked moneybox filled with cash and containing a lovely note of gratitude from the owner. My husband felt right at home, smiling an "I told you so" smile, while I had my mouth open in disbelief, rubbing my eyes every few moments to be sure I wasn't the one who was dreaming. Indeed, this was the real thing.

"Integrity, after all, is how one behaves when no one is looking, when only you know you did the right thing."

So what was the service message in all this? Had I lived in the Big City too long, becoming overrun with suspicion and cynicism? Had I lowered my expectation of the human condition? Was there hope that dignity, respect and honor were still alive and well in America?

Taking this even more personally, I thought about my own company, my own staff and my own way of doing business. Do I spend enough time and effort instilling trust and expressing gratitude or am I more often suspicious, cautious and protective? Integrity, after all, is how one behaves when no one is looking, when only you know you did the right thing.

Can you run a business trusting that, when given the opportunity, people will rise up and respond with honor? In my opinion, this concept is the ultimate service experience. Think about the statement it makes. Think about the message it sends to our children, who today are part of the Lost Generation. Think about the dream that could actually come true. Think about it, will you? When you do, I know it will serve you right!

# Let the beauty we love be what we do.

RUMI

# Judgment Calls

## Ability to Leap
## Tall Buildings Required

As employers, we help family and friends from time to time by offering their teenagers a place to work part-time or over summer vacation. It gives them real-life experience and gives us, the employer, an affordable option for handling the things we never have time or patience to do . . .

Hey! What are friends for, right?

Fast-forward ten years. There we all were, sitting around at a wedding shower for Julia, a now grown-up woman of 25 who was once a teenager working part-time for her mom's good friend Sara. Looking back and remembering Julia's teenage years, Sara shared a story none of us had ever heard before. Although it had happened ten years ago, we could see the conflict in Sara's eyes and hear the tension in her voice as she remembered the phone call that put her judgment on the line.

Sara owns a very high-profile and successful call center and fulfillment company. Even though Julia was just 15, it seemed like a no-brainer kind of job for her to answer the phones and take customer orders. After all, Julia was articulate and bright for her age, and talking to people came easy.

When the phone rang, the customer identified himself as a very important medical doctor who was calling from an airplane between destinations. He explained his order with a somewhat confrontational tone. You see, he wanted to order a sexual device that he insisted was for a medical purpose. Julia did her best to qualify the customer and the authenticity of his request, as she had been trained to do. The customer responded to her questions with indignation and rudeness, threatening to call his corporate affiliation if the order was not fulfilled promptly. Julia, seemingly unflustered, took notes during their conversation, assuring the client she would share the information with her boss and promising to call him back with a definitive answer regarding availability, delivery, cost, etc.

Sara, in the midst of tending to a million other details, noticed the crimson flush on Julia's face as she approached her desk. She listened to Julia's factual recounting of this unusual phone call and delicate challenge, and waited until Julia was quite finished describing and explaining the specifics. Julia was determined to act grownup and hold it together in a businesslike manner. And she did, until Sara went to the other side of her desk, took hold of Julia's hands, which were tightly wound around her pen and paper, and asked her how she *really* felt about the situation. Julia burst into tears, embarrassed, humiliated and quite obviously frustrated by the whole set of circumstances. She didn't want to be treated like a child, but she clearly felt like one right now.

Sara was now faced with several very important judgment calls. She had a customer who wanted something she couldn't imagine anyone wanting and whom she was obligated to serve. She also had an underlying responsibility to her larger customer, the corporate affiliation, which was responsible for almost 60 percent of her total business. Finally, she had a 15-year-old girl, the daughter of one of her dearest friends, who was in tears of confusion over what she thought was her rightful ownership to the sale, which, by the way, totaled several thousand dollars.

This request for a sexual device, the nature of which even Sara is too embarrassed to reveal to this day, also challenged her integrity as a businesswoman. She questioned her own judgment about saying yes to this inappropriate request, which at this moment felt more like a demand. Sara confessed to all of us listening to her tale that this was one of those complicated situations that test the heart and mind of a business owner, and she really didn't know what to do.

But Sara is smart, and she did know exactly what to do. She would never ask her staff to do anything she wouldn't do herself and, although Julia was determined to rise to the occasion and close the sale, Sara stepped in to do the dirty work. She called her contact at the corporate affiliation, provided the doctor's name and an account of his behavior, and explained the delicate balance of her own opinions about procuring such a device. Her corporate contact validated the marginal boundaries in this transaction and expressed appreciation to Sara for continuing her efforts to bring this sale to a close.

Sara then partnered with Julia, and together they created a strategy that served the customer and gave a boost to Julia's self-esteem at the same time. Julia did the research, the fact-finding, and, yes, the ultimate procurement of the device. But Sara insisted that she be the one to dialogue with this potentially difficult customer, knowing full well he would not talk to her the same way he might talk to a young girl. Together they closed the sale. Together they served the customer. Together they validated each other's contribution and integrity.

Today, Julia is a high-powered sales and service rep for a national corporation. She is also going to be a beautiful bride. Sara, her mother's dear friend, continues to leap tall buildings in a single bound to serve her customers. Julia looks lovingly at Sara and their eyes lock. You can see that in sharing this memory from the past, they both took a brief step back in time . . . remembering the vital lessons they learned and the judgment calls they made together.

# Many demolitions are actually renovations.

R U M I

# Failing
# to Serve

# If the Shoe Fits

*Businesses Exist for Customers,*
*Not in Spite of Them*

Most men hate to shop. Making a decision between brown and black can take hours. Big, powerful men become 12 years old when they shop for themselves, and each decision is full of uncertainty and confusion. So, when a favorite old-time customer of mine shared his customer service horror story with me, I could immediately sense his discomfort and vulnerability.

He was going to a family wedding and needed a new pair of shoes that matched his brand-new taupe suit. In a strip mall near his home, where he and his family shopped almost daily for one thing or another, he casually wandered into the neighborhood shoe store. Lo and behold, there was a pair of dress shoes with slightly scuffed soles, suggesting they had been there awhile and that several feet before his had worn them while customers considered making them their own. They weren't quite brown, and they weren't quite gray. He knew that unless he could hold the shoes right up to the suit to verify a color match he, too, would choose to leave the shoes on the dusty shelf.

The young girl working the store recognized him as a frequent customer who accompanied his wife and daughter, who shopped there often. When he asked to buy the shoes on approval, making special mention of the slightly scuffed soles, there was a completely mutual understanding that returning the shoes would not be a problem, right? Wrong.

Sure enough, the color of the shoes not only didn't match the suit, it also downright clashed. He confessed his embarrassment and nervousness about the whole ordeal to me as I patiently waited for the "horror story" part.

It seems that by the time he returned the shoes just one hour later, the friendly young girl who had taken such good care of him had been replaced by an older woman who happened to be the manager—and she was not having a good day. He sheepishly approached the sales counter with his bag and receipt in hand just as she slammed down the phone in irritation over another transaction. Make no mistake, this man runs a sizably profitable company that requires considerably powerful leadership skills. Yet at this moment in time this man felt his knees shaking and his voice quivering as he prepared for what surely would be a confrontational moment.

The manager breathed fire as she saw the scuffed soles of the shoes, accusing him of abuse and ulterior motives. She insisted no merchandise from her store would ever look like that and, besides, it was against store policy to sell shoes on approval. As he continued

> "Customers cannot be the interruption or the intrusion or the villain. They are people just like you and me."

to shrink into nothingness right before her eyes, she yelled at him and shamed him for his bad behavior.

Then something suddenly shifted inside him. He got taller, stronger and smarter, and, in an instant, he retrieved his voice and fully regained his power. Because this man is a nice man, a gentle man, he never lost his temper. Instead, he said in a somewhat firm and forceful tone, "Let me remind you, Ma'am, *you* are the overhead here . . . and *I* am the profit!!" She stood frozen in silence as he held out his hand for his refund, then quietly walked away, promising never to return to the store again.

Here he was telling me this story, wanting no more than personal validation and vindication, and here I am telling this story to remind us all that without our customers we have no jobs, no business at all. Customers cannot be the interruption or the intrusion or the villain. They are people just like you and me. There are stories, agendas and personality issues that accompany each and every transaction. Knowing this, our every effort should be to serve, making the buying experience a fun, comfortable event that builds memorable relationships our customers will want to share with other customers, so our business grows and grows . . . and where happy endings turn into new and prosperous beginnings again and again.

# I am only one, but I can still make a difference.

---

HELEN  KELLER

# Be Here . . . and Serve!

## *Rise Above Mediocre Service*

Why do people work where and when they don't want to serve? Too often, I see this "whatever" kind of attitude in the marketplace. As the customer, this makes me feel as if I'm an interruption, a burden to the person I thought was here to serve me, but who is really doing me a big favor by taking my money and time.

I was working on a personal art project, something I rarely give myself permission to do because of my many work projects. Just like in my professional life, I was pushing a deadline. It was close to midnight on a Saturday evening when I realized I needed positive and negative transparencies of several family photographs and note cards. Not wanting to wait another moment in completing the project, I remembered a 24-hour print shop down the street from my home. What a terrific service, I thought, acknowledging that there are obviously lots of people like me who want what they want when they want it—even at midnight on a Saturday night.

I gathered my precious photographs, love notes and special cards and carefully placed them in a large envelope, protecting them from the damp, cold night air. Sure enough, the lights were blazing in the shop, and I saw several other people busy at work inside as I quickly parked my car and scurried toward the open door.

I walked toward the front counter feeling full of gratitude for this accommodating service that was going to help me transform my art project into a family keepsake. I felt especially blessed when I noticed the title "Assistant Manager" imprinted on the gold name-plate of the person who was about to serve me: This was someone who knew what to do, someone who was in charge, someone who would care about my precious materials.

I waited patiently until it was my turn. The man ahead of me was trying to duplicate and size a tattoo design, which was as important to him as my materials were to me. Though he was someone I'd normally never consider myself to be "in the groove" with, I felt an immediate kinship with him. It was like we were in this *Twilight Zone* together, each of us holding on to our own reality.

Now it was my turn. I oh-so-carefully removed each piece from my envelope, explaining what I need-ed to the assistant manager so he could be my Service Hero and make all my dreams for the evening come true. Instead, he was distracted and totally annoyed by my requests. I watched him fumble through piles of papers from other projects while he copied my pieces, most of which he had to do twice because he did them wrong.

He was everywhere but with me. The potentially positive outcome this service experience could have had was completely lost. Left was the stark reality that this man, who supposedly was setting a leadership example in this company, clearly did not want to be working, let alone serving, in this print shop on a Saturday night. So why was he here, I asked him.

"Hey, it's a job," he retorted.

The saddest part of this sordid tale is that when I got home, feeling flat instead of elated, I started to assemble the pieces I had just reproduced and, sure enough, my daughter's graduation picture was missing. I immediately drove back to the shop but, alas, the overly efficient clean-up team had already picked up and disposed of all trash from the last hour's projects. We could not find my precious photo anywhere. The assistant manager didn't care about that, either. He defended, explained, blamed and quickly moved on to the next project that demanded his attention and burdened him in this midnight hour.

Yes, my project was completed. No, I never found my daughter's graduation photo. What could have been a juicy opportunity to serve and make someone's day instead became a less-than-mediocre performance. What could have resulted in an attitude of gratitude instead became an emotionally upsetting disappointment.

Dr. Carl Hammerschlag, a national speaker and local favorite, once said: "If you are going to be here, then *be here*!" If we choose to place ourselves, for whatever reasons and rationalizations, in a position that scares us, bores us or interrupts us from the things we really want to do, then shame on us.

"What could have been a juicy opportunity to serve and make someone's day instead became a less-than-mediocre performance."

———

# Keep your heart receptive and your eyes open, and everything you see will inform your work.

---

JANET MCCAFFERY

# Make It Right

## *Fix Mistakes First, Then Seek Lesson Learned*

Mistakes happen. When human beings are being human, it goes with the territory. I've read hundreds of self-help books that glorify mistakes as lessons learned. As an employer, I'm supposed to encourage my staff to embrace their mistakes so they can see first-hand the consequences of their actions and grow by making *new* mistakes.

Embrace mistakes? Never! Who am I kidding? I am still idealistic enough to believe in the "perfect" world where mistakes never happen and everyone lives happily ever after. When mistakes do happen—and they do—I don't embrace them one bit.

As a customer, my time and money are valuable resources, and I protect them absolutely. When I bought a $100 pen after much deliberation and I brought it home, ready for words of divine wisdom to spill out of the extravagantly fine instrument, I was not at all pleased when I carefully unwrapped the box, took the pen in hand and, lo and behold, the ink cartridge was missing. An oversight, no doubt, but in that moment of frustration, I couldn't think about anything but my anger. Now I would have to go back out in the heat, get in my car, fight the crowds for a parking space at the mall, schlep to the store and patiently (yeah, right!) place my pen back in the hands of the young saleslady so she could complete the job she should have done in the first place!

She was the only person in the store when I walked in, and she was on the phone for several minutes before she acknowledged my presence. When she finally put the phone down on the counter, I felt as though I was an interruption, and this phone call was obviously much more important than serving me. I remained somewhat calm, took a few deep breaths and remembered my forgiveness affirmations as I explained my problem to her, still trying to give her a chance to redeem her mindlessness. As she flippantly tossed her head with a "whatever" kind of attitude, I knew she didn't care whether I returned to this store or not.

What would have made me happy in this situation? I would literally have swooned if the young saleslady had first recognized the pains and efforts I had to go through because of her oversight. Then, I would want her to genuinely and sincerely take full responsibility for the error. It had not occurred because the factory sent it that way or because all the other pens automatically had the cartridge in place. It was strictly because she didn't verify the details necessary to complete a successful transaction. Lastly, I would want her to show her intention to resolve the problem by putting the

"As she flippantly tossed her head with a 'whatever' kind of attitude, I knew she didn't care whether I returned to this store or not."

SERVES YOU RIGHT!

beloved cartridge into my pen and perhaps even giving me a few extras to compensate me for my time and aggravation. I would then have left the store, coveting my new purchase and knowing I worked very hard to get it, but feeling the upset no longer mattered because I was so well served and so validated.

A happily ever after story? Perhaps. But this is a very tiny example of what happens in the marketplace when mistakes occur. Whether your bank takes forever to return your call regarding a loan approval, a furniture store delivers the wrong merchandise or your plumber forgets to show up for your appointment, it's their job to make it right once you've presented the problem. If they admit they care, if they accept responsibility and, most importantly, if they show their intention to resolve the issue, then they deserve the continued privilege to receive your business.

# There came a time when the risk to remain tight in the bud was more painful than the risk it took to blossom.

A N A I S   N I N

# Kindness Counts

*A Little Compassion
Goes a Long Way*

Indeed, in today's marketplace it is a rare event to be served, really served. Rude is in. Smiling is a sin. Mediocrity is the norm. Wouldn't it be a refreshing change to receive acknowledgment, validation and maybe, just maybe, a little compassion?

I was going to attend a weekend conference in Denver, beginning my sojourn in the afternoon after a jam-packed morning in my office. Having spent the morning clearing off my desk, returning phone calls, tying up too many loose ends and communicating with my managers, I squealed out of my office in a blur, arriving 45 minutes before my 1 o'clock flight.

As I stood hyperventilating at the airline ticket counter, I could see only the top of the ticket agent's head. I cleared my throat several times to get her attention. I even tapped my ticket on the counter. She didn't move. To prove to myself she was actually breathing and not just a strategically placed mannequin, I gently touched her shoulder. She raised her head, deliberately avoiding eye contact, and then quickly looked back down at the counter as she informed me the plane was delayed—indefinitely. Some maintenance problem, she mumbled.

Feeling powerless, I dragged my bags and my body to the nearest seat and tried to catch my breath. To diffuse growing resentment over the projects I could be completing at the office instead of sitting there waiting, I told myself maybe this was a good thing—a gift of time I didn't know I'd have, something I'm always saying I want.

Three hours later, an announcer droned that we could finally start boarding. No apologies. No explanations. No nothing. I originally was scheduled to arrive at 3:30 in the afternoon, in perfect time for the 7 o'clock conference kick-off. Alas, my plane touched ground in the middle of rush-hour traffic, and it wasn't until 6:30 that, breathless again, I finally arrived at my hotel.

I gave the cab driver probably the largest tip of his day, simply because I didn't want to wait for change. As I slid my heels across the hotel lobby floor, two young women behind the check-in counter were intimately engrossed in conversation. I was an obvious intrusion, interruption and annoyance, but that didn't stop me from my mission.

With charge card in hand, I blurted out, "I am here for the conference. My plane was late, and it took me forever to get here through all that rush-hour traffic! Could you, would you please check me into my room so I can still be on time for the 7 o'clock keynote?"

"Kindness counts, and so does the intention to serve."

SERVES YOU RIGHT!

One woman sauntered over to me like she was walking in molasses. I could tell she wasn't going to make this easy. First, she couldn't find my reservation, which I had made six months earlier. Then, when I requested a non-smoking room, she said she didn't have any left and reprimanded me for not specifying that need when I first made my reservation.

Never, not once, did she show an ounce of compassion, concern or humanness toward my stressful travel circumstances. I had just enough time to throw my bags into my room, brush my teeth and race three blocks to the convention—in the rain, I might add. Once I got there, exhausted and hungry from the stress and strain of the day, I finally relaxed . . . so much so that I fell asleep and missed the entire two-hour presentation.

What's wrong with this picture? As the customer, what could I have done differently to affect a more positive outcome? Certainly, I could have and should have released my grip over something that was obviously not in my control regarding the delayed flight and my insistence on meeting the 7 o'clock deadline. I could have and should have called ahead to the hotel, confirming my reservation and special needs and letting them know about my rushed arrival.

True, all true. But could these service people have done their job better? You bet they could have! Kindness counts, and so does the intention to serve. It takes so little to stand out, to make a difference and, yes, to serve you right!

# You've got to jump off cliffs all the time and build your wings on the way down.

RAY BRADBURY

# Answering the Call

## *"Slow Go," "No Show" Attitude Can Wither Business Growth*

Why is the hardest part of most any job just getting people to show up? When the customer is ready to do business, shouldn't the business be ready to serve?

I was ready, cash in hand, to develop a long-lasting relationship with a well-known nursery that would help me transform my yard into the picture I had in my mind. I love the desert, but I don't understand it. Its beauty differs from the lush greenery that thrives in the humidity back East. After almost 20 years in Arizona, I am still discovering new ways to appreciate its magnificence.

When we bought our home six years ago, the desert landscaping, with its promise of easy maintenance and year-round beauty, was one of the first things that caught our attention. The previous owner had invested time and knowledge to create a setting that had grown up over 25 years. Now it was up to us to take our yard to the next level. Off we went to our neighborhood nursery in search of the information we needed to make our garden grow.

Obviously, others had the same need because the parking lot was full. Clusters of people surrounded the front desk, and there were few service people to be found. That should have been our first clue. Being new to plant shopping, we strolled the grounds, making mental notes of the items that appealed to our senses. We waited patiently for service.

My husband was not as tolerant when, after 45 minutes had passed, we still were roaming the aisles waiting to be helped. By this time, we had made choices with absolutely no knowledge as to what would or would not grow in our particular yard. The few service people we saw answered our questions as they ran hither and yon.

"Where is hither and yon," I asked, "and how can I get there?"

This question finally stopped one young man in his tracks. When he saw my frustration and disappointment, along with my husband's percolating anger, he apologized most sincerely. His genuineness and intention melted our upset, and when he promised to have the owner call us to set up a home visit, I believed him.

I waited until the end of the week for the owner to call. When he didn't, I should have paid attention to my second clue that this place was not going to serve me right, no matter how much I wanted it to. I should have grabbed hold of the yellow pages and moved on. Instead, I called the owner myself. Surprise! Surprise! He took my call.

> "Business is cyclical, and when you burn bridges with attitude, arrogance and promises not kept, customers will remember for a very long time."

"Oh, thank you, Mr. Greenery Master. Won't you please take my money?" I asked him.

"Well, actually, Ma'am, I don't need your money," he said. "We are so busy we have all the business we need for now. Why don't you try us next year?"

"Was that a joke?" I asked.

"No Ma'am. This is business." Click.

I stood there holding the dead phone, wondering if I was stuck in a bad dream. Hey, I was the customer, and I had just been told to go away. What was wrong with this picture?

Now, I know you're going to say the customer is not always right. That's true. You're going to say he did me a favor by not taking on my business if he was beyond his capacity. Also true. You're going to tell me there are lots of other nurseries where I can get what I need, and I'll have to say true, true, true. But is this any way to "grow" and "cultivate" a business? This level of arrogance will be remembered by me and the hundreds of people I tell when times are not as good as they are now. Maybe then he'll have to "eat crow" or at least some "humble pie."

Couldn't the nursery owner have handled the situation with more courtesy and consideration, or at least a promise to put me on a callback schedule? Is that so much to ask, when I'm standing there with money in hand, ready to pay for services rendered? How about the roofer who gives you an estimate and doesn't return your calls to get the yes he needs to do the job? Or how about the yard man who only shows up once in awhile, ignoring the promised schedule? What about the painter who starts the job by dismantling your furnishings, and then disappears?

I don't get it. We are the customers! Our monies pay their salaries. Business is cyclical, and when you burn bridges with attitude, arrogance and promises not kept, customers will remember for a very long time. When these places hit the wall and start cryin' the blues, their businesses will be filled with echoes of long lost customers, and it will serve them right!

# The sole meaning in life is to serve humanity.

T O L S T O Y

# Being on the Same Team

*No Points Scored When Businesses
Ignore Customer Viewpoint*

I love to eat; therefore I must exercise. Spinning works for me. Riding a stationary bike in a class of 20 others, listening to loud rock & roll music, takes me far away out of my body so I don't feel the pain. It must work for others, too, because the "Battle of the Bikes" has been going on for quite a while now.

Hours before class—and some confess to the night before—spinners leave towels and water bottles to mark certain favorite bikes as being taken. Imagine the frustration for people who come as much as an hour before class only to find every bike has been claimed. Let me tell you, when you come to ride, no other workout will do!

When the club's management got tired of hearing high-pitched complaints from frustrated spinners, they decided to change the location of the sign-in procedure, an unintelligible rule that didn't solve the problem at all. Hey, who's listening to the customer here? What is the real message that is not being heard? It seems to me the spinning classes are a real hit, so why not offer more of them? Sounds to me like a *good* problem to have!

Rules and regulations are necessary for every business, but how many times do they get in the way of serving the customer? How many times are the rules more like the tail wagging the dog?

Last week I tried to order my "usual" from a chicken drive-thru restaurant. I was told the portions and menu had changed because it was better and more efficient for the restaurant staff. And how about the vitamin store that used to offer two-for-one purchases if you paid a fee to become a company member?

"Oh, that incentive doesn't exist anymore," the staff person informed me. "The owner decided to increase his stock value instead, and now we get the brunt of this new policy because we're the ones who have to tell the customer."

"Oh, that's swell," I said, as I ripped up my company card and walked out the door.

I don't get it. Without customers, there are no spinning classes, no chicken dinners, no vitamin purchases. Who makes up these rules? Why must it be a "them and us" situation? If management would simply talk to us, listen to us, see us as we see them, maybe they would notice that we're on the same team. We need each other.

I know bottom-line rules need to be considered, too, but these rules need to serve both sides of a transaction. Service enthusiasm builds the bottom line when the customer is truly the priority and the customer's feedback is respected. Management needs to walk the

> "I know bottom-line rules need to be considered too, but these rules need to serve both sides of a transaction."

floor, sit on the other side of the desk and experience business from the customer's point of view. What does the customer want? What services bring the customer back again and again? What does the customer value the most? Asking the right questions is the first step to getting the right answers.

# Attitudes are more important than facts.

CARL MESSINGER

# Showing Up

## Miss a Step and Competitors Will Cut in to Finish the Dance

My two-person accounting department was in major transition. We thought we had plenty of time after the support person gave us three weeks' notice, telling us she wanted to pursue a bookkeeping job on a Hollywood movie set. The following Monday morning, however, the overwhelmed finance manager crumpled up the project priority list and threw it on the floor as she indignantly walked out the door. My husband/partner, frozen in space and time, turned a whiter shade of pale as he watched her, wondering how he would do the weekly payroll along with daily deposits and sending out month-end statements. Clearly, we needed help and we needed it now.

I made a mad dash to the phone, calling as many friends and colleagues as I knew who could help me put a Band-aid on the sting of this situation, buying us time to find our new-hire replacements.

One friend, who has the business sense of a mastermind, directed me to a personnel agency that she swore had saved the day for her many times. As it turned out, this agency had been trying to get our business for years, so this was indeed an opportunity to show off in a very big way. Though our immediate needs were simple, they knew we had two full-time positions that needed to be filled plus the possibility of providing help for on-going seasonal business throughout the year. What we needed first, though, was a file clerk to get us organized so we could move forward.

Although no accounting expertise was necessary, I guess finding someone who would show up might have been the hardest part. By 8:30 the next morning, we had not seen a file clerk or had a check-in phone call from the agency. By 10 o'clock, my husband/partner started hyperventilating, so I called the agency and, in my most powerfully firm, no-nonsense voice, let them know we were losing patience while *still* waiting for their candidate to show up.

At 2:30 a young lady casually appeared on our doorstep. After two hours of slow-motion filing, we sent her home. The agency hemmed and hawed, blaming the employee market and offering some other procedural excuse. I called my friend to let her know about this lackluster performance so she would be aware for her future reference.

The good news is that quite a few other agencies recognized our crisis was indeed their opportunity. Let's face it: Providing exceptional service is all about solving problems. It's recognizing that customers have needs, and the sooner you can help fill those needs the more

"Providing exceptional service is all about solving problems."

likely your customers will remember you for their on-going business after their crisis is resolved.

Another critical aspect of exceptional customer service is continual follow-up. If the first agency had called us by 8:45 to confirm that their assigned person was there and working on the job, they would have known early on about the no-show and could have resolved the issue by staying present with us. Instead, our problem increased in magnitude with a day's delay and a lot of ill will and anxiety in the process.

As businesspeople, whether we provide a product or a service, showing up is the first step. Hey, it's a jungle out there, whether it's doing a dance to meet the heavy and varied tasks of running a business or doing a different dance to out-serve the competition in the marketplace. Count on it: If you don't serve—really serve—your customers, your competition will!

# I will act as if what I do makes a difference.

WILLIAM JAMES

# Being a Good Neighbor

*Excluding Nearby Customers
Can Have Far-Reaching Effect*

Aren't we lucky? We live in a city that many people pay thousands of dollars to visit . . . a city with more than 20 resort spas dedicated to indulgent service. And when you are burned out, fried, with nothing left to give to others, you give yourself the ultimate gift of a day retreat—an intermission from real life that potentially will renew not only the body, but the spirit as well.

A friend of mine and I recently claimed our Day of Indulgence. Wanting a new and different experience this round, we decided to choose a small, more "boutique" type of spa. We called two whose resort and restaurant facilities we had frequented throughout the year, and each was within walking distance from our homes.

The first call consisted of a conversation that lasted less than two minutes. Their spa was reserved exclusively for resort guests and members.

"No day packages?" I asked.

"No."

"You mean to say that those of us who live here 365 days a year, who eat at your restaurant and who suggest your facility to visiting guests . . . you cannot or will not serve us?"

"That's right," I was told.

I was appalled. Before I slammed down the phone, having been rejected by a staff member who clearly was not trained how to deliver this message, I assured her neither I nor any of my out-of-town guests would ever step foot on this property again.

The hero in this stressful saga, which was originally designed to eliminate my stress, was the Alvadora Spa at Royal Palms. Yes, serving their guests is their top priority; however, they want to serve their local neighbors as well. Instead of outrageous membership fees, they offer day packages based on availability. They want their neighbors to view the spa as their home just steps away from their home. They recognize that being a good neighbor helps balance out the seasons. They want people to stay there, and why wouldn't a good neighbor recommend them to their out-of-town guests? Being a good neighbor is a two-way street, and Royal Palms is open-armed in living this principle.

The extraordinary level of service I experienced at the Alvadora Spa in the six hours I was there rejuvenated not only every cell in my body but also my faith in service enthusiasm! Heather did not have a scheduled power walk that morning, but she made one happen in a flash when my friend and I inquired. A young man parking cars on the property saw me walking from the

"The extraordinary level of service I experienced at the Alvadora Spa in the six hours I was there rejuvenated not only every cell in my body but also my faith in service enthusiasm!"

fitness center to my car and offered me a cold bottle of water, just like that. The server during our two-hour lunch patiently accommodated our dietary needs and slow-as-molasses pacing.

Then, at long last, it was time for my "ritual treatment," during which I was scrubbed and wrapped, rinsed with three overhead showers, then scrubbed extra clean under a trough shower followed by a gentle water massage under a rain shower. As if that was not enough, I then soaked in a hot, bubbly mineral bath, munching on almonds and dried apricots, drinking cold bottled water, and enjoying the sight and smell of fresh flowers everywhere. The tub perfectly supported my back as I luxuriated, staring out the open window to a private patio and roaring fireplace. Whoever designed the space had seen and experienced the whole process through a customer's eyes. That's why everything was so utterly perfect.

Months from now, as well as on special occasions, I know exactly where I want to be, and you can bet I will tell everyone I know—both in and out of town— where they *must* go when they want and need a mindful experience that approaches nirvana.

As a wake-up call to the rest of us who have a seasonal business, it's critical that we remember to take very good care of our year-round clients because being a good neighbor is what good service and good business are all about.

# When what we are is what we want to be, that is happiness.

MALCOLM FORBES

# Going the
# Extra Mile

# Little Things Make a Big Difference

*Perks Take Business from Ordinary to Extraordinary*

Mass production, mediocrity and day-to-day standard operating procedures put most companies and most customers on automatic. We've learned to accept less, settle for the ordinary and tolerate the "whatever" kind of attitude. Shopping offers little more excitement than any other errand on the to-do list, and this means the thrill is gone for hundreds of former "shop-till-you-drop" shoppers.

With all the sameness in today's marketplace, it takes little to stand out from the rest. It's the little things, the unexpected pleasures, that sharpen the competitive edge between businesses that operate like everyone else and those few where customers are appreciated just a little bit more.

It's so easy really: Like the florist who keeps a bucketful of free flowers near the front door with a note saying, "Take one. This bloom's for you!" Or the car dealer who washes and cleans your car after you've had it serviced. Or the store that offers to wrap your gift purchases at no extra charge. Samples of sweets, demos in grocery stores, a free movie on your birthday—all are efforts intended to send the message that your business is important, that you are an appreciated and valued customer.

**"It's the little things . . . that sharpen the competitive edge."**

Sometimes this concept is alive and well in what we might consider to be unlikely places. Buying athletic shoes is hardly at the top of my list of favorite things to do. In fact, unless my sock bottom shows through the tread on my rubber soles, I usually insist the shoes I have are still wearable.

One day, however, I wandered into a small privately owned athletic store to register for an upcoming running event. As I was filling out the application, another customer came in looking to buy new running shoes. The salesperson, after a warm greeting, asked the customer some pertinent questions as the pair moved toward a treadmill in the back of the store. Free of charge, the salesperson videotaped the customer running, paying attention to whether his feet rolled toward the inside or outside and coaching him on how to change his form to avoid injury. She then fit him with the running shoe that would best serve his needs.

As I watched this exchange, the level of service inspired me. I wanted some of that, too. And, hey, I really did need a new pair of running shoes, right?

As customers, we settled long ago for compromised service, including petty pricing for anything extra or specialized. We kept quiet when we should have spoken up. We accepted when we should have refused.

Thankfully, extraordinary service is out there, sometimes when we least expect it, just waiting for us to notice. By frequenting the isolated few instead of the mediocre masses—and then sharing these astonishing service stories with family, friends and co-workers—we can nurture the hope that this goodness will be contagious, that businesses who value customers with acts of kindness will grow and prosper. For now, these are the precious few who deserve more of everyone's business.

In this volatile business of ours we can ill afford to rest on our laurels even to pause in retrospect. Times and conditions change so rapidly that we must keep our aim constantly on the future.

WALT DISNEY

# Put the Shine On!

## *Strive to Be the Exception to the Perception*

Every profession or industry has customer perception built into it. Think about all those networking introductions when everyone is wheeling and dealing with handshakes and business cards. What is the reaction when you tell them what you do? How do you react when they tell you what they do?

"Oh, you are a physician. How nice!"

"Oh, you are a lawyer. I'm sorry to hear that."

"Oh, you design, host, market, repair and repair again web sites and computer technology. Well, you and everyone else I meet lately."

But right up there with the worst possible career choice—right next to selling used cars—is the person who sells insurance. It's like having a built-in handicap.

Meet Karlene Arnold. Thirty years ago, a woman decided to sell life insurance more as a dare than an opportunity. Karlene was given six months to "survive." She not only survived, she thrived. She was so successful she was chosen "Rookie of the Year." When she eventually decided she "didn't want to talk about death," she transitioned from selling life insurance to selling health insurance because she knew she could really make a difference "amongst the living." My company is one of her many success stories.

I remember a time when I stood hopeless and paralyzed as I stared at my group insurance renewal notice, hoping my sweaty palms would melt away the hardcore truth and bottom-line decision that seemed imminent. A 30 percent increase! Thirty percent!! How could my small business, still reverberating from September 11 and an unstable economy, afford such an increase? It couldn't. I was angry at the gouging. I was frustrated by the bureaucracy. I was saddened that I would have to adjust our company policy because I knew how deeply this news would affect my managers and employees.

Karlene was already "on it" when we spoke the same day.

"Rest assured," she bellowed into the phone, "this is what I do best. Just let me do my job. This is how I get to make my difference."

And that she did. Karlene pared my initially heart-wrenching 30-percent increase down to 12 percent, allowing me to deliver an entirely different message in my staff meeting than the one I had dreaded when the renewal notice first landed on my desk.

Karlene puts a shine on the perception most people hold about insurance companies, agents and brokers. Many of us believe they are the "enemy," making bazillions of dollars at our expense. We believe insurance

> "Karlene pledges never to lie, deceive or cheat her clients or carriers, and she embraces her role as the bridge between the two."

people can't be trusted because of hidden agendas and half-truths. Karlene pledges never to lie, deceive or cheat her clients or carriers, and she embraces her role as the bridge between the two. She works the variables, she "sells" the client to the carrier and she manifests win/win solutions.

How can each of us create a shift and put a shine on our own profession? What historical and experiential perceptions do most people have about your industry? How are most people or companies in your profession doing business? How can you do your business differently? How can you be the exception to the perception in your industry?

Take a look at your competitors. What do they do that you can do better? Take a look at what doesn't work in your industry. What can you do to reverse the outcome with more service, better communication and absolute integrity?

Just like Karlene Arnold does for the insurance industry, we all have the opportunity to deliciously surprise our customers when we exceed their expectations, shatter a negative belief system and, as a result, put a shine on our career of choice.

# When you lose, don't lose the lesson.

D A L A I   L A M A

# Small Town USA!

## *Bringing Back Memories of When Service Was King*

Road trips give you a chance to see small towns at their best. Visiting a small town can be a trip back in time, where life moves slower, people know their neighbors, and there is an underlying layer of pride about what people do and who they are.

My husband and I took an up-close look while we traveled the back roads to and from a Colorado vacation. For as long as we've been married, we've pledged not to frequent franchise and chain stores whenever we have a chance to choose Mom & Pop instead. Thank heavens small towns are where Mom & Pop are still very much alive.

We started out quite early one day, knowing we'd find a perfect breakfast somewhere down the road a piece. We were looking for charm, good home cooking and some feeling of adventure.

In Circleville, Utah, we were drawn like magnets inside the doors of the Thunder Moon Craft and Ice Cream Parlor. Mother and son, Ida and George, were there to greet us with huge smiles. Every inch of the place was original and handmade: the wood-planked floor; the varnished wood booths; the hand-painted regional drawings; the horseshoe salt, pepper and napkin holder centerpieces; and, of course, Ida and George themselves.

Ida was a small, yet visibly strong woman. Her eyes sparkled, and she spoke with an ever-present smile. She proudly announced she was a great, great, great grandmother, and that she and her granddaughter made most of the knitted crafts in the shop while George had done must of the handiwork and paintings we saw all around us. George sat confidently on one of the counter stools, a man I'd guess to be in his 40s, wearing tight jeans and cowboy boots. His face was both tough and tender. His real passion, he confessed, was good old-fashioned, made-from-scratch cooking. That was our cue because we were starving by then and ready to eat everything we saw on the handwritten menu.

Choosing was the hardest part. Among the listings were apple dumplings, George's secret spiced French toast and eggs with half a pound of homemade sausage or an eight-ounce rib eye steak. The prices took our breath away: $3.95 to $5 across the board!

Barry couldn't resist the flapjacks. George said he'd start by making up two because they were as large as a dinner plate. If Barry could eat all that, he'd make up a third, and his breakfast would be free! George beamed with this grand offer because no one had ever been able to eat more than two of his monstrously delicious flapjacks.

George also informed us that he hand-cut his own meats and loved to watch his customers gasp at the portion size. We were no different from all the others he had served when our breakfasts arrived. We couldn't get enough. It tasted so good, and there was so much of it.

George and Ida sat there watching us savor every bite, proud they had exceeded our expectations with a high-quality meal at a ridiculously modest price. They shared stories about their family, their heritage and their annual August barbecue bash. By the time we finally waddled out of there back into the real world, we were carrying a piece of homemade blackberry pie, chocolate baklava and a made-from-scratch chocolate malt right out of my childhood. We wanted to take Thunder Moon with us, to keep the experience alive for just a little while longer. Of course, I tried not to think of the extra sit-ups and long-distance runs I was going to have to do to pay penance for all this eating pleasure.

As I looked back and saw George and Ida waving good-bye to us in the doorway, I was reminded of their pride and how privileged they felt to serve us. What a unique gift of gratitude they gave us. I flashed forward to the Big City, where I saw myself face-to-face with an ATM machine or a store clerk who rarely looked up, let alone thanked me for my business. When was the last time we had received more than we paid for? How long had it been since a prideful glow had beamed from someone who was serving me?

With one last glimpse of George, Ida and Thunder Moon, Barry and I renewed our promise to visit the back roads, patronizing the small shops and restaurants where the American dream is still breathing . . . and where it's all about good, old down-home service.

"As I looked back and saw George and Ida waving good-bye to us in the doorway, I was reminded of their pride and how privileged they felt to serve us."

# The world is a dangerous place to live; not because of the people who are evil, but because of the people who don't do anything about it.

ALBERT EINSTEIN

# A Personal Touch

## *Creating a Unique*
## *Shopping Environment*

I love to shop. I've been told I've earned a black belt in this sport, considering the miles I've walked in stores, malls and out-of-the-way boutiques that others would never travel that far to see. Because I am a Super Service Seeker, I notice every effort that welcomes me, creates a mindful shopping ambiance and presents merchandise in a tastefully aesthetic way. I usually don't have a lot of time (or money) to indulge in this shopping sport of mine, so when I've designated time and identified a specific need, I want my shopping experience to be as satisfying as indulging in a once-in-a-while hot fudge sundae.

Anita is such an indulgence, and she knows just how to serve her lady clients. Having operated a retail store for many years, she recognized the nearly impossible task of recruiting and retaining good staff. Anita therefore decided to serve her ladies with a completely new approach that operates without a store or employees.

She travels twice a year to three home-base locations in Toronto, Chicago and (lucky me) Scottsdale. Through word-of-mouth only, her clients make appointments to visit Anita at her home. The door opens, and Anita stands there smiling a warm smile that starts in her eyes. She's usually dressed in one of her own smashing ensembles. Inside, Frank Sinatra and Ella Fitzgerald croon soothing music in the background, and fresh flowers are carefully placed around the living room and the bedroom, which now becomes my very own spacious dressing room. She brings me a large chilled water served in a wine goblet as I start to unload my purse and car keys, beginning to feel right at home.

Anita has done her homework. Remembering what I bought last season and knowing my preference for certain styles and colors, she has gathered several pieces of clothing she knows I will like. I wallow in all this personal attention, feeling as if, for the moment anyway, I am her most important client. She has designed her own line of clothes and accessories that mix and match into countless combinations, justifying her somewhat inflated prices. But, hey, this experience is worth every penny compared to the congestion of inventory and people in most stores. I am the only one in this space at this time, and Anita gives me her individual attention as we coordinate, eliminate, and pick and choose what works best for my budget and me. Anita is honest and candid with her opinions, reminding me why some of her clients have been coming to her for more than 16 years!

Unlike clothes in a store, whatever I don't buy will probably be gone forever. Her next appointment might buy the size or color I'll reconsider tomorrow, and once

"In our fast, go, go, go pace, consumers hunger for an indulgent intermission, and they are willing to pay for it."

Anita leaves for her next city, she'll be gone until the next season. She manages to tote her inventory, replenish her stock and serve as many as 30 clients in a 10-day stay, generating in excess of $50,000. Not bad, huh?

Anita has figured out a unique way to do business. She provides a quality product with astonishing personal service. She offers beautiful, comfortable surroundings that relax and nurture her clients. She has no employees, no advertising costs, no leasehold improvements and no overhead except three homes in places she likes to visit. Anita has found a way to simplify and glorify the shopping experience. As one of her many satisfied clients, I anticipate her call just as the new season is about to begin. Now that's good business, don't you think?

Retail stores can learn a lot from Anita. Her focus on her customers and attention to detail in creating a "shopping environment" that nurtures her client base have created "raving fans" who love her service. In our fast, go, go, go pace, consumers hunger for an indulgent intermission, and they are willing to pay for it. Why? Because it serves them right!

# Do you want to be safe and good, or do you want to take a chance and be great?

JIMMY JOHNSON

# Here Comes the Bride!

## *Personal Service Makes Shopping a Joy*

Even those of us who are age-old feminists dreamed, as young girls, about the day we would become brides. It's the "fairy tale come true" syndrome, when the world stops and stares at you with loving eyes while you stand in glorious beauty as The Bride, glowing in white light, more feminine and womanly than at any other time in your life.

I wanted this state of bliss for my one and only daughter when I became a MOB (also known as Mother of the Bride), and we began the search for the wedding gown of her dreams. This time together would surely be a mother/daughter moment each of us would always remember.

Rachel flew in from California specifically for this gown-shopping marathon, and I was ready for her. I had done my homework. After talking with several other MOBs and brides, I had identified four places to shop.

It's been said that 90 percent of the time the first dress you put on wins your heart forever, so I knew my best shot needed to be our first stop. Several people had told me about a family-owned business that had been dressing brides in beautiful gowns and providing extraordinary service for more than 20 years. Sure enough, the first gown and veil Rachel put on had us both in tears.

We took snapshots from every perspective so we would remember every detail from this day forward. Rachel was fairly certain this gown was it, but the saleslady, who was the owners' daughter, insisted she not only try on many other gowns in the store, but that we shop in other stores as well. I didn't remember having to make so many decisions about sleeves or no sleeves, detachable trains or bustle trains, white or ivory colors, short or long cathedral-style veils when I was a bride.

And then there were the costs! As the MOB, you hope and pray you and your daughter won't fall in love with a gown that could easily surpass the food budget at the wedding. That's when you start paying attention to offers for free alterations and a customized veil at no charge if you pay for your gown in full. Our young saleslady reminded me about their special services as we were leaving her store and heading to the next shop.

Our second shop was just a few blocks away. We had a difficult time finding a parking place, and when we finally arrived we were corralled into a tiny reception area along with five or six other people. A gold cord spanned across two retail counters that were heavily merchandised with pricey mementos, from guest books and fancy garters to engraved wineglasses. Oh, yes, weddings are a very big business. I saw swarms of brides, moms and bridesmaids checking all this out, and I thanked the heavens none of this interested my daughter.

"Just the gown, Mom," she reminded me. "Just the gown."

We couldn't cross into the wedding gown den until we filled out a form. We were then assigned a saleslady, who could easily have been someone's grandmother. Nice touch, I thought. Rachel and I, along with our saleslady and her assistant, filled up an oversized dressing room with armfuls of petticoats and gowns. We were told sweetly that photographs were forbidden. With no real privacy, Rachel undressed and followed instructions: Arms straight up, dive head first into layers of petticoats, stand straight and tall, and tell me what you think. Rachel was clearly overwhelmed with this approach and getting more claustrophobic by the minute. It was time to move on.

We stopped next at a smaller and more personable store. They did not have as large a selection as the last two, but their gowns were much more unusual. Their salespeople didn't hover, but they stayed very present, servicing Rachel outside the dressing room as she tried on gown after gown. By now, we were both thoroughly confused and uncertain as to which gown, if any, would be her choice. Time for lunch, I said, like a good mother should.

Though we had driven all over town, there was one more store Rachel just had to visit because a friend had bought her gown there. It was 4 o'clock on a Saturday afternoon, and there was frenzy inside the shop. People filled every corner and every dressing room, with salesladies running barefoot between them all. We finally were rushed into a room and given the

> "They offered services at no additional charge and had opened their store on a day they were supposed to be closed."

rules: No pictures and no gown changes without a saleslady being present. We were told to expect additional charges for alterations or customized additions, as well as the possibility that our favorite gown just might be discontinued in the near future if we didn't order it today. As the saleslady scurried out the door, I noticed a sign that said, "We'll share your tears if your wedding is cancelled, but the gown you buy is yours." My heart sank at the thought of this scenario for any bride, and I was angry at them for suggesting the possibility . . . it was a fine-print policy that would have been better suited on the final bill of sale, not in dressing rooms where dreams were in progress.

That night, Rachel fell asleep in my arms from exhaustion and restless confusion. I, too, dreamed of one gown after another. The good news is that Rachel pounced on my bed Sunday morning before the sun came up: She was sure, absolutely sure, her choice was the very first gown she put on. She just needed to try it on one more time before her plane left that evening.

As a MOB, I learned how to leap tall buildings in a single bound, and this desire of Rachel's would be no easy task because the store we needed to get into was closed on Sunday. We knew we had a slim chance because Rachel remembered her saleslady had scheduled a fitting for another bride sometime on Sunday. Pure persistence and determination ran through my veins as I psychically tried to guess when the fitting could be. At 2 o'clock that afternoon, I drove to the store on a mission. Rachel sat in the car with her hands covering her face in embarrassment as I pressed my nose to the dark windows, tapping on the glass with my key. Sure enough, as is the case with many family businesses, the owners were there. They greeted us warmly, making us feel we weren't the only neurotic bride and MOB who had gone through this tumult. They turned on the lights, and let Rachel have at it.

Within 15 minutes, Rachel was in my arms again, in total joyful bliss. I marched up to the counter, checkbook in hand, blessing this sweet family whose shop stood apart from all the other stores we visited. They offered services at no additional charge and had opened their store on a day they were supposed to be closed. This was where I wanted to do business. This was the place I wanted us to recall when remembering the precious day we found Rachel's wedding gown. This was the customer-oriented business I knew would serve me right!

# Courage is contagious. When a brave person takes a stand, the spines of others are stiffened.

BILLY GRAHAM

# Service with a Smile

## *Accelerated Service Drives Routine Appointment to Point of Purchase*

Taking my car in to be serviced is right up there with having my roof fixed: It generally costs more than I hope, the reward seems intangible, and the service itself is usually an inconvenient annoyance I just have to tolerate.

So there I was at 7 o'clock on a Tuesday morning, driving the freeway to my car dealership for a routine service appointment. As I pulled into the service area, a bright-eyed young man wearing a tuxedo shirt and bow tie opened my door and greeted me with a genuine smile. What a surprise!

My service provider appeared within moments, handing me the keys to my loaner for the day as I watched my car being whisked away for the operational procedures that needed to be done.

Clean. Fast. Efficient. I was impressed but in no way ready for the next seductive treat awaiting me. After all, it was only 7:30 in the morning, and already I felt as though I was dreaming up the whole experience! For me, the ultimate Super Service Seeker, this indeed would be my kind of dream come true!

As I said good-bye to my service provider, I asked her to point me in the direction of my loaner car. I fully expected an older, smaller and clearly more used version of my almost 3-year-old car, which was now being serviced. Instead, she pointed to a brand-spanking-new car with fewer than 77 miles on it, which just happened to be in my favorite color!

"Really?" I squealed. "That's what I'm driving today? Really? Oh, my!"

I hadn't even had my first cup of coffee, yet I felt my whole body buzz with excitement. She helped me adjust my seat and mirrors. Cautiously, I turned on the radio, anticipating the heavy metal or rap music that had blasted out of every other rental car I had ever had. But, no, even that detail had been addressed: With the press of every button I heard a favorite classical, jazz or oldies station. I hugged (yes, hugged) my service provider good-bye, rearranged my entire day to have as many appointments as I could *out* of my office and drove into the sunrise to live happily ever after.

How brilliant this level of service was! Was it pure coincidence or could they have suspected that by the end of the year I'd probably be choosing my next new car? Was this service enthusiasm a dream . . . a seduction . . . a genuine effort? Who knows, and who cares?

All I know was I felt special, important and worthy. That morning had been unlike any other Tuesday morning I had experienced in a very long time. And, after test-driving a brand-new model for an entire day,

> "Was it pure coincidence or could they have suspected that by the end of the year I'd probably be choosing my next new car?"

I stopped at the showroom floor when I returned to pick up my car, which, by the way, was ready on time and at the charge I had been quoted earlier. I made my interior and exterior color choices and set a time line for delivery of my next new car. I was hooked and grateful to be sold!

Then I started to think about what had just happened to me: How the company took a routine experience and turned it into a service celebration! I wondered how I could do more of that in my business. How can you do more of it in yours? The surprise treats, the small indulgences from start to finish in every transaction can knock your customers' socks off and bring them to your door for more every time, any time!

# The person who has
# no imagination has no wings.

MUHAMMAD ALI

SERVES YOU RIGHT!

# Gotta Go!

## *Restroom Conditions Speak Volumes to Customer*

Let's talk about the unspeakable . . . the unmentionable . . . the forgotten customer service area of every business, restaurant or public building. I'm talking about bathrooms, also known as restrooms or Temples of Relief. Whatever they're called, the point is that many businesses forget to provide cleanliness, comfort and beauty within these frequently visited facilities.

There are lots of ways to go, excuse the pun. I was in one of my favorite restaurants in a newly renovated mall, a definite high-traffic spot. Toilet paper was strewn on the floor and everywhere else, except where it should be. All four stalls were missing this most precious commodity. Puddles of water surrounded the sinks, and there was no soap in the dispenser. As much as I used to visit this local favorite, I haven't been back since.

I was treated like royalty in the restroom of yet another favorite Italian restaurant. Not only did they create a beautiful space for me, complete with mouth-wash to clean away that yummy taste of garlic, but I also learned to speak a few words of Italian during my five-minute visit. Now that's clever—and demonstrates a great effort in customer service. When I returned to my table, I had to share my "restroom experience" with my dinner group. Even now, when we talk about where we want to "go," we all remember this place for its great food, great service and great bathrooms!

Public places like theaters, airports and malls gear their restroom image to whatever is most efficient. These public bathrooms have toilets that flush them-selves and regular cleaning crews to fill stock and keep cleanliness next to Godliness.

When I visit restrooms in office buildings, I'm often surprised when I need a key to get in. Is it because of security, loitering or out-and-out rudeness? What mes-sage does that send? Why should any human be denied access to a bathroom?

Speaking of bathroom denial, here's a true story with an added lesson in the punch line. A mother and her 3-year-old stopped at a bank to use the restroom—and you know when you're dealing with a 3-year-old, you don't have a whole lot of time. Yet the Bank Lady not only refused them access to the bathroom, but asked them to leave as well. Perhaps it was because of the way they were dressed. Perhaps it was because this was the bank's corporate location, and they weren't accustomed to dealing with children. Perhaps it was because the Bank Lady had an argument with her own children that morning.

Mother and child left the bank all right, but not before their mission was completed. The 3-year-old

> "When I visit restrooms in office buildings, I'm often surprised when I need a key to get in. Is it because of security, loitering or out-and-out rudeness?"

simply couldn't wait a minute longer and "let loose" on the expensive rug in the bank lobby. The mother simply couldn't wait a minute longer to close her account with this bank, and guess what? Her net worth turned out to be a considerable fortune! Now that's what I call instant karma!

Department stores challenge customers to find the restrooms. Usually they are tucked away in a far corner of the store, behind the luggage department or near what the store calls its customer service area. Unfortunately, you have to ask at least eight salespeople along the way to help you find the facilities or at least point you in the right direction. What a waste of our time and theirs!

Yes, there are rare occasions when bathrooms are not only clean and accessible, but beautiful as well. Soft lighting, fresh flowers and appropriate music let customers know the company's management has spent time and effort considering all their customers' needs. It's always in the details, isn't it? It's one thing to say you serve the customer and quite another when your actions say it for you.

So whether you call it a bathroom, a restroom or a Temple of Relief, it is indeed another level of service, another opportunity to treat the customer like a welcomed guest. And our job, as the customer, is to communicate our appreciation to management and to encourage our friends and family to shop there, eat there and do business there more often. These establishments are at your service because they know just how to serve you right!

# You can't shake hands with a clenched fist.

GOLDA MEIR

# Officer Friendly Lives!

*Compassionate Service Transcends
Lack of Competition*

When the Chief of the Richmond (as in Virginia) Police Department called to see if I'd conduct a two-day seminar on customer service for his senior managers, I was speechless. Customer service consciousness seemed like an unlikely coupling with the police, especially when newspapers were filled every day with police brutality stories. That's hardly what I'd call good customer service!

I remember reading one article that said the New York police were being forced to take etiquette classes and another article that quoted then-President Clinton's concern that the frequency of recent police misconduct charges was undermining the fight against crime. Clinton proposed improved training (customer service, perhaps?) to restore the bonds of trust between the public and law enforcement.

My contact with the law—and thank heavens my only experience with the police—occurred on a rather base level when I got a speeding ticket, thanks to a camouflaged photo radar truck. When a hidden camera is your only connection to the law, you're not likely to bond and build a relationship of trust.

Unlike so many other businesses that could potentially lose their customers to the competition if they don't provide the best quality service, a police department has no competition. They're the only game in town, and why should they care if their only job is to protect and defend us? What could I possibly say to this group that would inspire them to change their thoughts and behavior? How would I ever get them to understand the importance of listening and validation? How could I encourage them to be vulnerable when everything they've been taught as part of a paramilitary organization is exactly the opposite? This sounded more like a *Mission Impossible* setup, where I would surely self-destruct if I did not choose to take this on.

The Chief himself made me reconsider. Not only is he an extraordinary visionary who is ego-less and fearless at the same time, but he also walks the talk. I always want to stand next to powerful people.

When he was brought into the Chief's position four years ago, the police department was underfunded, undernourished and demoralized. He cleaned up the facilities and working conditions, increased compensation, computerized police cars, bought new uniforms and built his team with inspiration and opportunity. Now he thought it was time to demonstrate the "right stuff" to the community they served, and he wanted me to reinforce the department's role as service providers to his senior managers, who would then communicate this to their staffs. The Chief was committed to doing whatever it took to create a world-class, state-of-the-art police department that provided excellent customer service, and he thought customer service training was the next step on the journey. I guess that was my cue.

Our two days together were jam-packed with information and interactive experiences. I started by asking each person to share why the police force had been his/her career of choice. Usually the stories went back to childhood and included a role model with plenty of inspiration. They then shared their vision for customer service in their specific areas and for the department as a whole. We role-played actual case studies, and here again the Chief insisted on playing hardball.

One case was clearly an issue of racial humiliation, and when a black officer offered to play the part, the Chief stood up defiantly and reminded the group and me to dig our heels in and get real about taking big-time risks to assure greater growth. Having a white officer feel the shame in this case would surely be a more gripping lesson.

Toward the end of the first day, there was a semblance of alignment regarding the need and desire for better customer service. The homework assignment that evening called for the managers to create for themselves and their departments new titles that exemplified their customer service mission. Think about that. Choosing a new identity meant accepting a new way of working and being because once they declared who they were, they had to be it! The Chief, in his usual high-stakes way, followed up on my homework assignment by stating these new titles would be printed on their business cards, stationery and any other written communications, announcing to all that members of the Richmond

**"Choosing a new identity meant accepting a new way of working and being because once they declared who they were, they had to be it!"**

Police Department were serious and definite about how they would serve the community and each other.

The next morning the energy had stepped up several levels. Anticipation and excitement filled the room. As the managers stood tall and introduced themselves, there was a sense of pride and commitment to the declarations: Director of First Impressions, Leader of Ultimate Understanding, Chief Energizing Officer, Head Wow-er, Chief of Enthusiastic Employees, Dream Resource Hunter, Head Buck Stopper and so many more. The morning session ended when the Chief announced his new title: Chief of Enormous Opportunities. Indeed.

I think about the members of the Richmond Police Department often. I think about their courage, not only when they are doing their jobs fighting against crime, but also the courage it took to be in that room for two days, exposed and vulnerable, and the courage necessary to so positively embrace change. These are human beings who truly care about making the world a better place. Their commitment to improve their relationship with the citizens (customers) they serve and each other (customers, too) is honorable and heartfelt. It was truly a privilege for me to witness their customer service awareness as it unfolded and blossomed. Remembering their standing ovation still brings tears to my eyes because they helped me realize a dream: the dream to make a difference.

# Consider the
# Human Element

# Throwaways

*Let's Get Personal—Even
If It Is Business*

Vendors are people, too. We've all been there at some point in our career development, perhaps as recently as yesterday. When a colleague friend of mine returned my call about a project we were working on together, I noticed his voice sounded flat, almost lifeless. He was reluctant to share his story until he trusted my understanding that he was not complaining or whining, but simply deflated in a moment of defeat and frustration. I recognized the symptoms because I've been there many times myself, and I knew a good listener could work wonders.

His company was one of two finalists in a national search for a public relations proposal for a very large, well-known East Coast company. Not only was the allocated budget plentiful, but the added prestige in winning this account would also move my colleague's company up several notches in public credibility. He worked his team, he invested more than 90 hours of his talent and energy, and, sure enough, his company was one of two remaining. He enrolled his main contact at the big company as his cheerleader. He tweaked his proposal and invested more time and money in following her suggestions. He was cautiously optimistic.

One week away from the promised date for a final decision, my colleague and his team lost sleep wondering, hoping and worrying whether they would indeed win this account. The date came and went. No word. He called his contact at least three times, leaving voice mail messages gently inquiring what the final word was, but there was no response.

Finally, ten days after the promised announcement date, my friend got a two-sentence e-mail that said the decision indeed had been made last week to go with the other company and that, because her schedule had been so jammed, she hadn't had time to return his calls to let him know the bad news. My call came a few hours after that, and now it was perfectly clear why my colleague barely had breath left to answer the phone.

He confessed that as sorry as he felt in not winning the account after coming so close, what was particularly defeating was the way he was told, the way he became invisible—no courtesy, no compassion. He and his company were mere throwaways in this dramatic scene. He had not only lost the countless hours of time and thousands of dollars he invested in this proposal, but he also lost the feeling of being seen as human.

I know, I know. It's a jungle out there. Business is business. But service is a two-way street, and you get back what you give. We are all vendors, and we are all customers. Investing in relationships and common

"...after coming so close, what was particularly defeating was the way he was told, the way he became invisible—no courtesy, no compassion."

courtesy can't be a bad thing . . . in fact, what else is there?

When we start treating people like throwaways in our world of business, are we sure this same attitude doesn't transfer over to our personal worlds as well? Do marriages become throwaways? Do our children see us treat others this way? Do we use e-mail and voice mail as cover-ups for the real thing, the real connection that allows one human voice to connect with another? Maybe it's as simple as living and learning that good old Golden Rule, treating others as you would want to be treated. Maybe it's as simple as that, and wouldn't that make our world a better place all around? You bet it would!

# You gain strength, courage and confidence by every experience in which you really stop to look fear in the face … You must do the thing you think you cannot do.

ELEANOR ROOSEVELT

# Coming of Age

*Machines Continue to Advance,*
*but Humans Still in Charge*

Okay, I admit it. I'm technophobic. Call me old-fashioned, but I still write with a pad of paper and my favorite pen. I still send thank-you notes and birthday cards instead of e-mailing them.

Typewriters have been replaced by laptops, and soon there won't be any phones connected to the wall. When I decided to throw out my answering machine and go to voice mail, it was a very big deal. I counted on my tape recorder and hands-on daily message retrieval, but, alas, the advantages of electronic voice mail seduced me enough to cross over. With voice mail, I could check my messages at the office, at my home, at my home office and on my cell phone. When did we get so full of our "accessibility importance" and ourselves that we needed all these communications every instant?

Over the years, I slowly began to trust this new-fangled voice mail process . . . until last week when my reputation was on the line. I'm a person who believes in returning all phone calls promptly . . . I say it and I do it. Imagine my surprise when a colleague approached me at a Wednesday morning business meeting and asked why I hadn't returned her call from Monday regarding an important communication I needed to know about. How strange, I thought.

The next day, I saw my doctor and anxiously inquired about the results of a recent lab report. She informed me she had left a detailed message on my voice mail a few days ago. Now I was really puzzled.

The answer to my confusion came when a friend who was moving her business shared a story about wanting to hire a moving company. She had called the company, but no one had returned her calls. She later found out the mover's voice mail had been down, and he never even knew about all the business he was losing. Ah ha! I knew technology couldn't be trusted!

I followed that lead and, sure enough, when I called my carrier I was casually informed that my voice mail service had been down for days. I had umpteen messages just hanging out there in the techno-ethers, including the ones previously mentioned. My reputation and on-going business communications had been jeopardized. Life seemed so simple before technology, but in the name of progress it has taken over our lives.

I know, I know. Technology is our friend. We've come a long way. Today we have the ability to store, connect and process with one click by one finger on one hand. But has technology crippled our world with a dependency that holds us hostage?

I've been told my business could not survive without computers, yet crashes and glitches have the power

"Life seemed so simple before technology, but in the name of progress it has taken over our lives."

to paralyze operations. They also have costs in the thousands. And what about the dollars that continuously flow into this bottomless technological pit because equipment you buy today is obsolete tomorrow?

When my IT guy explains to me how and why this or that problem exists in our internal program, then proceeds to tell me how much more money it will cost to fix or update, I understand every third or fourth word he says. He is a nocturnal being, speaking a totally unfamiliar language using words that have no meaning to me. He tries, really tries, to talk slowly to me, waiting patiently for me to digest and integrate this foreign information. All I know is that I'm not in control here, the machines are. Everything is connected to everything else and, when one part goes down, every department—every system—stops while we wait and wait some more for resolution and/or a technological miracle that will allow us to continue working our businesses.

I stretch my comfort zone daily, trying as hard as I can to embrace this technology craze and bless it for the gifts it gives. Yet I remind everyone within earshot not to get too comfortable in this world of gigabytes, .net frameworks and crystal reports. Humans are still the variable here; therefore technology, just like real life, is prone to error and breakdown. Yes, we humans are still in control.

I held a moment in my hand, brilliant as a star, fragile as a flower, a shiny sliver out of one hour, I dropped it carelessly. O GOD! I knew not I held an opportunity.

HAZEL LEE

# Speedy Recovery

*Spirited Service Restores Order*
*and Renews Faith*

When you own a seasonal business that focuses on gift giving, there's nothing quite like the month of December. The truth is, our company produces half its yearly sales volume in the three weeks leading up to Christmas. Staff projects, strategy meetings and system improvements begin in January and progress through to December 1, as we continually seek ways to be more efficient and effective in serving our customers.

This Christmas was our 24th holiday season. My staff members measure their tenure by how many Christmas seasons they've worked, knowing each year brings its lessons and legends. You'd think after 24 years we would have our systems down, flattened, in check. But, alas, there's always more to learn, especially when so much of what we do is homemade and handmade.

There are more hands-on people than automatic, pre-dictable machinery. It's the human factor that brings the challenge—and the glory—to what we do, especially at Christmastime, when we're working 24 hours a day, seven days a week.

On the day before Christmas Eve, I walked into my office a bit later than most of the previous days, feeling our month's marathon winding down. I felt the same energy as I walked through the various departments in the building, until I was nearly bowled over by Tommy, our warehouse supervisor. He was breathless, and his eyes were big and round, darting from one corner of the warehouse to the next. Although he's a whole lot bigger and stronger than I am, my hand gently pressed the middle of his heaving chest as I asked him to tell me what his panic was all about. Tommy was trying heroically to rescue a situation that never should have happened.

Weeks ago, a customer of many Christmas seasons had called to place this year's holiday order, which included one of the largest and most expensive gifts we offer. It was a hand-painted 30-inch Santa sleigh, chock full of ornaments, candles, picture frames and, of course, oodles of fresh cookies. This gift had been such a hit throughout the holiday season that, indeed, his order claimed the last sleigh to be found on our shelves. The problem was that somehow, somewhere, part of the sleigh frame had been broken and badly nicked and scratched. Though it was packaged beautifully, the customer was in a fit of rage when he saw the condition of his gift—a gift he was giving to his most important client, who happened to have 13 children.

How this negligence happened, how my staff packed up defective merchandise (albeit a great presentation), and how the gift got through a minimum of three quality-control checkpoints were issues that needed to be addressed. The immediate need, however, was to serve this rightfully enraged customer by figuring out what I could possibly do to remedy the situation a day and a half before Christmas.

Tommy followed me forward as I approached the customer with forced confidence. The customer could barely speak and would not make eye contact with me because he was so angry, frustrated and, yes, disappointed. He insisted there was nothing I could do to make this right. The huge Santa sleigh was the gift he wanted: It was the gift he ordered and nothing else would do. Although I offered him several other gift options, he stood by the door, looking out at cars passing by, and barely acknowledged my feeble attempts to please him.

Because Christmas is indeed the Season of Miracles, I had one card left to play—one I thought would be the solution to what seemed like a tragic ending for our season. Kathy is my merchandise manager, and she's been known to work many a miracle over the seven years we've worked together. If anyone could pull a rabbit out of the hat, Kathy could. I also knew she was a saver, a collector of one-of-a-kind containers from seasons past. She would know exactly what to do.

Somehow I convinced the customer to give me another chance. I promised him, assured him, guaranteed him that by 9 o'clock tomorrow, Christmas Eve morning, he could come back to pick up a gift as huge and grand as the Santa sleigh was supposed to be. My intention was all he heard and, perhaps because of our successful years of serving him, he believed me.

Kathy remembered a photo shoot three years ago, from which she had tucked away a larger-than-life 36-inch Santa boot that had held my then 3-week-old

"It's the human factor that brings the challenge ... to what we do."

grandson perfectly for our featured catalog cover. Once Kathy did her magic, this boot would be the miracle we needed to put a smile on our customer's face . . . and the faces of those 13 children.

The next morning our staff gathered 'round to watch Kathy and I stand front and center as the customer approached our front door. He was barely cordial, not really expecting much. All eyes were on the customer as Tommy carried out the huge, overflowing Santa boot. In that moment of saving grace, watching the transformed expression on our customer's face, we all felt the spirit and miracle of Christmas!

Our customer was speechless, but this time for all the right reasons. The tears in my eyes matched his. This was what the holidays were all about. This was why, many years ago, I opened my business doors: to learn and grow from my mistakes, to serve my customers absolutely, and to make a difference . . . especially to those 13 children on Christmas Eve.

# Sometimes your joy is the source of your smile, but sometimes your smile can be the source of your joy.

THICH NHAT HANH

# Turn It Off

## *Cell Phone Convenience Shouldn't Put Human Contact on Hold*

We are all multi-taskers. Time being the most precious no-return commodity, we pack our days and minutes into dense activities that complete multiple functions in the same minute of time: We listen to conversations on the phone while clicking out e-mail messages . . . we travel down the freeway at 70 mph, talking or, worse, dialing numbers into our cell phones . . . we carry on business discussions as we buy our groceries. We are so "not in the present" moment. Unfortunately, the ultimate goal to create more "free" time has ended up costing us more in heart attacks, highway accidents and dysfunctional families.

It's the family part that breaks my heart. We're the adults. We're the ones who need to set the example because, sure as thunder follows lightning, our children are our mirrors.

It was dinnertime on a Wednesday night, and I stopped in for a bite at a casual family-style restaurant. Across the aisle from my table, a young boy about ten years old was pushing food around his plate while his dad talked and laughed on his cell phone, obviously in another place and time. The boy never looked up from his plate. If he had raised his head just once, he might have seen me inviting him to sit at my table to tell me all about his day at school or maybe about his bike ride home that afternoon. Even as his father paid the check and headed for the door, his cell phone conversation consumed his attention, sending his son the message that he clearly was not his dad's priority.

That experience stayed with me for weeks. Then I saw this behavior repeated in reverse, and I knew I had to speak up.

It was a beautiful spring day when the temperature from a gentle breeze just tickles your skin with its coolness. Having lunch in an outdoor café was a must. My husband and I sat for a long while, enjoying the chance to watch people and each other. In walked a 14- or 15-year-old girl with her grandmother, who was reaching out for the young girl's arm. Unfortunately, she didn't notice her grandmother could use a touch of support or affection because she was plugged in to her cell phone conversation. And so it was for almost their entire meal together. Before dessert, the young girl went to the ladies room, and I realized I had little to lose in talking to her.

As we both washed our hands, I mentioned I had noticed her having lunch with her grandmother and remarked about how special that time must be. I told her how close I had been with my grandmother, how

> "Unfortunately, the ultimate goal to create more 'free' time has ended up costing us more in heart attacks, highway accidents and dysfunctional families."

SERVES YOU RIGHT!

blessed I was to have had her for so many years of my life and how, though she lived to be 97, I wished with all my heart I could have lunch with her just one more time on a beautiful day like today. I reached out and touched this young girl's shoulder, seeing her eyes get full and wide, knowing she got my heartfelt message and knowing she was right here, right now, at last.

Make no mistake: I am the queen of multi-taskers. My goal, in fact, is not only to multi-task, but also to figure out a way I can actually *be* in two places at the same time. I'm as guilty as everyone else when it comes to cell phone driving. Even though I have hands-free cell phone access, I'm still surprised when I arrive at my destination, having no idea how I got there.

When it comes to being with people, though, I turn my cell phone off. And that's true of business meetings, too. As tough as it is, I try to keep my computer keyboard from clicking away in the background when I'm on the phone in my office. It's a matter of respect, as well as better business.

Nothing is more precious than being with someone in present time, because present time is truly all there is and what in this world could be more important than the human being sitting across from you?

# Energy must amass over time before perceivable change occurs.

A PHYSICS PRINCIPLE

# Empowering
# the Troops

# Good Help is Hard to Find

## *Business Suffers When Staff Fails to Apply Common Sense*

Coupon clipping can be a full-time job, and businesses that use this form of advertising must know it works. Coupons can attract new customers into a business by sparking a need, along with an inviting discount that makes the first purchase feel like a deal. Coupons can also be a gracious thank-you offered to existing customers who have patronized the business so they can enjoy an appreciative discount toward their next purchase.

Seems like a win/win result to me, but unfortunately some businesses do not empower their front-line staff to think on the spot. Because staff members lack training and empowerment, they lose sight of customer-service goals, often exercising poor judgment, rigidity and power plays that cost businesses the customers they wanted to attract or retain in the first place.

My son and daughter-in-law, married three years, are trying to budget and save wherever they can. With a $5-off coupon on purchases of $20 or more, they returned to a stationery store from which they had ordered personalized note cards several times before. They made their choices, tallied the total cost and showed their coupon, celebrating the $5 savings on their $40 purchase. Then the sales clerk noticed the coupon was two days past the expiration date.

What to do? What to do? Follow the rules explicitly or exercise some good common sense that would serve the customer in the short run and the company in the long run? Unfortunately, the clerk decided not to accept the coupon. Can you believe this lack of vision? She turned away $40 to save $5 and, worst of all, lost good customers in the process.

Why do companies shoot themselves in the foot like that? I realize expiration dates are a good thing. They send an immediacy message, a customer call to action. There have to be boundaries and rules and regulations . . . I know all that.

But thinking is allowed on the job, and empowering front-line staff to think things through and use good judgment rather than operating on automatic shouldn't be asking too much. As a business owner, I believe that if the coupon brings me a new customer or thanks a regular customer, who cares what the expiration date is! The coupon worked, and that's what's important.

I know, I know. Good help is hard to find these days. When my newspaper wasn't delivered this morning and we called to get one, the regional manager delivered it himself within 15 minutes. He sincerely apologized, saying carriers were hard to come by and

"Because staff members lack training and empowerment, they lose sight of customer service goals."

it was nearly impossible to fill slots and deliver good customer service at the same time.

Every restaurant, every shop, every business I frequent has a "help wanted" sign in the window. There's a price for these good times we're experiencing. But does that mean we should settle for less? Lower our standards? Not expect our staff to think and feel during customer transactions?

True, mediocrity is the norm and rude is in, which spells "opportunity" for those isolated few who refuse to compromise and who stay committed to motivating and inspiring their staff to think, serve and make decisions. They know service based on attitude and common sense not only builds the bottom line, but also gives back so much in return—knowing you've truly served the customer, made the difference, created relationship and brightened someone's day. It's really that simple.

We act as though comfort and luxury were the chief requirements of life, when all that we need to make us happy is something to be enthusiastic about.

CHARLES KINGSLEY

# Please Take My Money!

## *Spirited Service Opens Door to Success*

When technology prevails over cold, hard cash; when newly schooled high-tech managers haven't learned their people skills; when there is a missed opportunity to be the hero for the customer, it makes you wonder why a business would try to attract customers at all.

It was Wednesday afternoon, and there I was, waving my $20 bill while I tapped at the locked door of the music store. I had just called from my office because I couldn't stop humming a song I had heard earlier that morning on the radio. I had to have that CD! Piles of projects and appointments tightly scheduled for the rest of the day just wouldn't have my full attention unless I had that song playing in my office.

"As business owners and creators of vision, do we translate that vision by empowering our staff to make decisions based on the immediacy of the moment?"

I called ahead to the local CD mega-store, known nationwide for its vast selection and inventory. Sure enough, this was indeed my lucky day. I asked the salesperson over the phone to please leave my do-or-die CD at the front counter so I could leave my motor running as I made a mad dash in and out of the store. She assured me my beloved CD would be waiting.

And I could see it, just at the corner of the counter near the register, as I pressed my left cheek to the cool glass of the front door. But why was this mega-structure so dark in the middle of the day? Where was the salesperson who had assured me just moments before that I would be another of the store's happy customers? I tapped on the door insistently until, at long last, a young 30-something manager appeared and very calmly walked toward me. I enthusiastically flashed my $20 bill in full view, thrilled that this young man would be my hero, if only he would please, please open the door and let me pay for my precious CD, getting me back to my office before my 2 o'clock appointment. That's when I heard the news: The computers were down, so the store was closed until the problem was resolved. Closed tight. End of story.

"Oh, that's okay," I said. "I don't even want my change . . . just take my money and please, oh, please just give me that CD on the corner of the counter over there."

"Well, no, Ma'am. I can't do that."

"You can't? Why not?" I shrieked, hearing my voice go up several octaves.

"Just can't. That's all there is to it," he said, as he closed the door and locked it.

I stood there speechless as I watched him walk into the darkness of the shut-down store, leaving me on the outside, estranged from my coveted CD.

Later that day, after picking up my CD at a different music chain, my business-owner mind started to ramble through the ramifications of this event. As business owners and creators of vision, do we translate that vision by empowering our staff to make decisions based on the immediacy of the moment, or is our staff so committed to policy and procedure that customers are forgotten? Is it fear of making a mistake or overstepping authority that scares off the risky decisions, or is it the accountability factor? Do we encourage our staff to think—and feel—on the job . . . or is that not in the job description?

So many employees are "on automatic" or have a self-absorbed "whatever" kind of attitude. Is it possible to find spirited service that reaches out to the needs and concerns of the customer? Imagine how refreshing it would be to be served by someone who cares, someone who really wants a customer to be more than satisfied—not just one time but every time. Bottom-line results are guaranteed with that kind of service enthusiasm from an employee who knows how to come through in a pinch and has been empowered to do so.

For a long time it had seemed to me that life was about to begin—real life. But there was always some obstacle in the way, something to be gotten through first, some unfinished business, time still to be served, a debt to be paid. Then life would begin. At last it dawned on me that these obstacles <u>were</u> my life.

ALFRED D'SOUZA

# Who's Guarding the Gate?

*Ineffective Front-line Support
Compromises Position*

A friend of mine was in the middle of a meltdown. Known for his repressed anger and occasional outbursts of rage, his wife had gently suggested he attend an afternoon "Learn to Manage Your Anger" seminar. That evening he told his wife he actually "enjoyed" the seminar, and after sharing his experience with a few of his buddies, they agreed they should pursue the idea of hiring a therapist for group anger-management sessions. My friend volunteered to make the initial call to the therapist to confirm fees and scheduling.

The therapist's assistant answered the phone. When my friend asked to speak to the therapist to possibly schedule the group's first session, the assistant hemmed and hawed. In flustered responses, she told him she was the one who usually did the scheduling, but because the doctor was terribly busy she didn't feel capable of setting this appointment. She had no idea when the doctor would have a moment to return my friend's call or fit a session into his already maxed-out schedule.

My friend tried to stay patient in pursuit of some resolution. After several rounds of frustrating non-communication, my friend's blood pressure started to rise until the assistant finally promised to call back within the next two days. Two days came and went without a call.

That's when my friend had another meltdown. How could he possibly learn to manage his anger when the professional he hoped would help him had chosen an incompetent "gatekeeper"? So, he lost his temper . . . and his intention. He reported back to his buddies and, in pure frustration and annoyance, they decided to give up on what initially had been a brave idea.

Doctors' assistants and executive assistants have a lot of power, and that power has a tremendous influence on a customer's perception of the business. Inefficiency and ineffectiveness can be as damaging as the other extreme of arrogance and self-importance. Does your assistant embrace your vision of how you want your customers and staff to experience you? Are you sure?

I had an assistant once who, in my mind, was the ultimate achiever in serving my needs. I often wondered if she had learned to read my mind because she was so good at anticipating my requests. She was fast, effective and very present during a time in my career when I was often out of the office, traveling on sales calls. We were the perfect team—or so I thought.

A brave staff member quietly cornered me in the hall one day to tell me what no one else would dare. It seems my superstar assistant had become confused about whether she was the assistant to the president or the assistant president. Using my name as her shield, she had been barking all sorts of orders and directives to my employees and, yes, to my customers as well. After I verified this information, I confronted her in my office. She then went to lunch and never came back. I didn't have to fire her—she fired herself.

Make no mistake: Assistants and support staff can be the most valuable resource of any company. How else can managers and leaders move a company forward? How else can we accomplish all that we do? Without the integrity and efficiency of support staff, we, as leaders, are literally stuck on a very short leash. However, we have to be oh-so-careful that the people we choose to implement the policies, procedures and systems we create will work for the benefit of our customers and the rest of our staff. Double-checking that perception just might be a worthwhile wake-up call!

# You are built not to shrink down to less but to blossom into more!

OPRAH

# When You Care Enough to Give Your Best

*Recognition of Individual Contribution Empowers Employees*

While I was in New York on business, I ate at a restaurant that had been highly recommended. Although the ambiance was inviting, the hostess was more concerned that our name had been inadvertently omitted from her reservation list than in giving us a warm welcome. And although my dinner was magnificently presented, my food was tepid rather than served hot.

When the manager genuinely asked how I enjoyed my eating experience, I decided to take the opportunity to actually tell him the truth instead of dismissing him with the usual "fine, just fine." (As a self-appointed Service Enthusiast, I've learned over the years that unless I'm asked for my opinion and feedback, it generally is not considered help, and therefore not always welcomed or well received.) His response to me was refreshingly candid: "These are the very things that make a good restaurant a great one . . . and we are simply not there yet. The hardest part of my job is getting my staff to care."

How do we inspire our employees to "autograph their work with excellence"? How do we build a quality-control factor into our company's culture? How do we instill accountability and responsibility that doesn't involve finger-pointing blame? Here's some food for thought to sink your teeth into:

1. Your outside reflects your inside. Your staff is a reflection of you: your moods, your work ethic and your values. The way you embrace excellence or just get by is exactly how your employees will demonstrate their performance. As the owner/manager, modeling service enthusiasm is the best way to inspire it in others!

2. Consider the now nearly universal catch phrase: "What's in it for me?" Why should an employee (or anyone else for that matter) care? What's in it for them? Since mediocrity has become the norm, affirmed with a regular paycheck, why should anyone offer more? Because "giving makes you rich," that's why. Unless an employee actually experiences the joy of serving and helping others, customer service exists solely as a lip-service concept. As owners/managers, we need to create opportunities for every employee to be a hero with customers and/or co-workers. When an employee realizes every moment offers a chance to serve, it won't be long until that feel-good feeling becomes a habit . . . a habit we as managers/owners want to reinforce.

3. Personalize your product/service so each employee "owns" his or her contribution. Recognizing that every

> "Recognizing that every step in greeting and serving customers is a 'moment of truth,' employees begin to see how each person contributes to each part of the process."

step in greeting and serving customers is a "moment of truth," employees begin to see how each person contributes to each part of the process. To really drive this point home, ask each employee to imagine that this product/service is for his or her own mother, husband, wife or best friend. Every Christmas season, when Cookies From Home welcomes 100-plus temps to its various 24/7 shifts, we ask them to pretend that each tin of cookies is being delivered to someone they really care about and to imagine how wonderful they would feel knowing every scrumptious morsel and every package was prepared and delivered with perfection.

We're talking enrollment and empowerment here. We're talking about creating service enthusiasm junkies. We're talking about a work environment that recognizes the more someone gives the more they get back in personal reward and recognition.

# Even if you are on the right track, you'll get run over if you just sit there.

WILL ROGERS

# Attitude Is
# Non-Negotiable

# Fuel for Body and Soul

## *"Attitude of Gratitude" Offers Hope for Renewed Work Ethic*

It had been a long and challenging day. I was exhausted and starving. Not sure if I had the energy to lift a fork, my husband suggested a nearby salad bar for a quick and easy dinner bite. It was difficult to get excited about lettuce, cucumbers and bean sprouts, but I didn't have the strength to argue. Food was fuel, and I was running on fumes.

My salad actually looked good enough to eat: full of reds, yellows and greens along with a diversity of crunchies for added taste appeal. We sat among a roomful of diners who, like us, hovered over their plates, mouths open wide, chewing non-stop. Every table was filled with "food people," from toddlers to seniors, eating to get their money's worth.

Then I saw Carlos, a robust young man with a contagious smile. Carlos was busing tables as if we were in his own kitchen at home. He was doing this less-than-pleasant job with an ambassador's attitude. I continued to watch him. He engaged everyone he served with laughter, conversation and quality attention. He was ever present with drink refills, extra napkins or a clean plate for yet another round of good eating.

Carlos managed to create relationships within moments, and truly he was genuine with every exchange. As his customers waddled toward the door, they waved Carlos good-bye like part of the family. Carlos would smile as he cleaned the explosive mess left on the table, the floor or the booth. Was Carlos real? I had to find out.

"I love my job," he said. "I have young children at home, and I know that dinnertime is sharing time. My job is to make people feel comfortable here. I make a lot of friends."

"Oh, my," I said. "You are quite special, Carlos. You understand the real meaning of service. Do you have any clones?"

I don't think he really understood my question, but I know he understood my acknowledgement! In further conversation, he proudly shared that he had one other job and he was also going to school. Two jobs, a family and school . . . talk about a long and challenging day!

If Carlos could have such an "attitude of gratitude" and could continue his larger-than-life presence with his customers while he cleaned up habitual food-fight messes at 8 o'clock on a Tuesday evening, how could I possibly complain about my long and challenging day sitting at my desk or walking around my office solving the usual day-to-day problems of running a business? I was humbled.

> "Carlos managed to create relationships within moments, and truly he was genuine with every exchange."

When it was finally time for me to "get horizontal" and close my eyes, I realized my dinner "event" provided salad as fuel for my body and Carlos as fuel for my soul. He inspired me. He energized me. He gave me hope for a finer work ethic. He reminded me that it's not *what* you do; it's *how* you choose to do it.

# Think of other people. Serve other people sincerely. No cheating.

DALAI LAMA

# Working on Purpose

*Creative Expression Turns Job
into Spirited Livelihood*

Recording your own radio spots can be a dangerous thing. As "free talent" representing the identity of your company, you can mistakenly fall in love with the sound of your own voice, which can hurt sales . . . unless you are blessed with the right producer at the keyboard.

Although I'm sure there is considerable talent at the local stations where I spend a lot of my advertising dollars, I fly to San Diego to work with Kevin Dean at KYXY because he makes me sound like I know what I'm doing. Besides providing stand-up comedy to relax me when I first arrive at the station, he makes me think we're a team, ready to go into the ring to co-create the best 60-second spot ever to be heard on the airwaves. Yeah, right!

We both know Kevin is in complete control, and my job is simply to show up and surrender. He serves me without my even knowing it. He edits my long-winded copy with his red pencil and controls my timing, taking out a few extra breaths to bring my spots in at exactly 60 seconds, not a millisecond more or less. He coaches me on inflection, articulation and pitch throughout the entire process. His patience far exceeds mine when, after 45 minutes, I'm still trying to get a 60-second spot just right or, heaven help us both, finish a 10-second spot in one long breath. I usually leave the studio within an hour, feeling like a star and relegating Kevin to the process of choosing background music, the final touch that will make my radio spot the one that calls an entire listening audience to action! Kevin makes it all look so easy but, after many years of working with him, I now know better.

Kevin has been with KYXY for 10 years, and that's staying power in the radio industry. He has survived four general managers and four program directors, yet grows in spite of the changes and challenges that come his way. He delivers his smile, quick wit and divine patience not only when he produces radio spots with clients like me, but also when he co-hosts the morning show and local traffic report in the wee hours before sunrise, when most of us are still in dreamland.

Kevin is a three-time award winner for his morning traffic report. Unlike most outside services hired by stations to do this job, Kevin keeps his listening audience—who might be stuck in a freeway pileup—entertained and informed as an integrated part of the morning show. Kevin is the first to admit he is not a performer; he just likes to talk to people and make them feel good. The service level he provides his

"Most of us operate only at a minimal capacity of our potential, unsure what it is we are really meant to do with our lives."

customers is based on his commitment to make people feel good . . . no matter what.

When was the last time you woke up in the morning with a mission to make people feel good . . . no matter what? When was the last time you opened your eyes to a new day, knowing that every ounce of your being was ready to serve on purpose? Most of us operate only at a minimal capacity of our potential, unsure what it is we are really meant to do with our lives. Any road will do when you don't know where you're going. But Kevin knows where he's going because he still loves what he does every day . . . and he can't believe he gets paid for it, too!

Work is supposed to be a creative expression of spirit. We're here to make a difference, to be the difference in repairing and rebuilding our world, a world leaking economic instability, corporate mismanagement and a shortage of visionary leaders. Humans like Kevin Dean remind us that people can live their lives with purpose, mindfully choosing attitude and presence in the workplace. Humans like Kevin show us how to serve from the heart, inspiring hope for us all.

# A very important part
# of the joy of living is the joy of giving.

WILLIAM BUCK

# Be Here Now

## *"Just a Job" Attitude Smothers Spirit*

Trade shows are a form of endurance training. Whether you are an exhibitor or a buyer, you've incurred considerable cost, invested concentrated hours and developed a very focused agenda of goals and objectives. Both sides of the equation are ready to do business and take full advantage of this scheduled opportunity, right? Not this time.

I've played both roles in this arena, but this round I was the buyer attending a gift show. I'm sure I walk millions of miles on unyielding concrete floors at these shows. I look up and down every aisle, first right, then left, searching for that one bit of interest, that one extra ounce of energy that will slow me down long enough to consider actually walking into a booth for a closer look. I carry the list of items I need to find, I schlep my bag full of vendor catalogs and samples picked up as "definite maybes" along the way, and I devote great effort toward quieting the mental chatter stimulated by sensory overload to my brain.

I look for refuge. I look for someone who wants to sell (serve) me. A smile would be nice. Eye contact from someone who really "sees" me would be even nicer. Alas, most exhibitors I see are so bored with their product and what they do that they are literally asleep at the wheel, missing every potential buyer who walks past their booth. I see them engaging with other exhibitors, talking on their cell phones or simply staring blankly into space. Hey, there was one booth full of toys and games, and the sales guy was tucked away in the corner, sound asleep! If *they* aren't excited about what they do, why should *I* be? After all, showing up is only part of the job . . . being present is a whole other concept!

Trade shows are not the only place you see such a blatant combination of apathy and boredom. This lackluster attitude can be found in department and retail stores, restaurants, medical offices . . . my heavens, it's everywhere! We all spend so much of our lives at work (eight to ten hours a day, 40+ hours a week, 170+ hours a month, 2,080+ hours a year), and we all have chosen what it is we want to do with our lives, right? Right! So if we are going to be here, let's really *be here now!*

If work is "just a job," aren't we cashing in a huge chunk of our lives for the "security" of a paycheck? This attitude costs us our spirit, and our spirit is priceless.

This is it! This moment—right now—will never be again. Do we want to sleep through it? Why not step out onto those skinny branches where the fruit is and taste the juice that reminds us of our aliveness!

Work is the expression of spirit, and that spirit loves to serve, loves to connect and loves to make a difference. How can "dead eyes" serve customers? They

> "If work is 'just a job,' aren't we cashing in a huge chunk of our lives for the 'security' of a paycheck?"

can't—and they don't—yet this is mostly what we see. Mediocrity is the norm. What an invitation that is! Service and spirit can be the competitive edge for any individual or company. Whatever the product, whatever the event, whatever the social and/or economic circumstances, the intention to serve gets the attention of every buyer . . . and don't you think that's what makes the *real* difference to the bottom line?

# Fall seven times, stand up eight.

JAPANESE PROVERB

# Identity Issues

# Do You Know What You Are Really Selling?

## Vision and Foresight Put Identity in Clear Focus

Most people think going to a gift show is one big excuse to go shopping. Most people think we buyers pick out whatever we happen to like best. Somehow, it all comes together, miracle of miracles, when product arrives, is merchandised and, sure enough, is bought by our customers. Then we all live happily ever after, right?

The reality is that, as buyers, we have the awesome responsibility of maintaining the integrity of our company's vision. Our buying decisions affect so much more than simply buying merchandise. You bet we need to know marketplace trends and seasonal themes, but, more importantly, we must know who we are as a company, how we are different from our competition and why customers come to buy in our store. What is the underlying feeling or need we can satisfy better than anyone else? What are we *really* selling in our company?

Let me be specific with examples we all recognize. What is Kodak *really* selling besides film, cameras and photography supplies? Kodak is selling memories and heartfelt moments in time. Each poster or 60-second commercial tugs at our hearts and moves us to tears in record time. Families, tenderness and moments we relate to and want to remember always . . . that's what Kodak is selling!

And what about Allstate? "You're in good hands with Allstate." Sure, they're selling insurance, but what they are *really* selling is security, safety, protection and peace of mind. Who wants to talk about insurance? No one. But we all want and need peace of mind, don't we?

Besides gazillions of dollars in lipsticks, eye shadows and mascara, what is Revlon *really* selling? Revlon offers all us women who are victims of our advertising culture not only beauty but also hope . . . yes, *hope* is what Revlon is selling more than anything else.

So what is it *you* are really selling? What is the vision, the plan or the story that encompasses why you are in business and why customers should buy from you? Once you're able to clearly identify this critical piece of information, this concept will permeate everything else you do, right down to the name of your company, how you market your company, how you merchandise your store, how you staff and train your personnel, and how you buy and sell your products.

Ask yourself continually: How does this communicate to the customer what I'm *really* selling? Is this consistent with my company's image, niche and message? Any and every decision you make must be in alignment

> "You bet we need to know marketplace trends and seasonal themes, but, more importantly, we must know who we are as a company."

with everything else or your customer will get confused, frustrated or—even worse—bored with trying to figure out who you are.

In these challenging economic times, it is more important than ever to know who we are, how we are unique in the marketplace and how we can better serve our customers with consistently reinforced messages that will bring them back to our store again . . . and again . . . and again.

# The work of our heart, the work of taking time, to listen, to help, is also our gift to the whole world.

JACK KORNFIELD

# Hold on to Your Edge

*Finding Need and Filling It Elevates Crowd Member into Leader of the Pack*

It was my birthday month, and dear ones closest to me know I love to receive and, when necessary, exchange gifts from my favorite department store. At this department store, unlike others, returns and exchanges usually are hassle-free and even welcomed with a smile at any sales counter.

On this Tuesday night, however, my favorite of all favorite "shopping arenas" had lost its edge. As I approached the first sales counter with my gift to exchange, I saw only the top of the salesperson's head as she pointed me in the direction of another department. The salesperson there took a short minute to look up from her inventory sheet to tell me I needed to go up to the next floor to exchange my gift. This next salesperson was not only unfamiliar with the merchandise I was returning but—horror of horrors—she also had not been trained to process a return transaction from an out-of-state store.

Okay, maybe this simply was an off night. But the final blow came as a crashing disappointment when I wandered throughout the deserted aisles of clothing and accessories, birthday money in hand, and did not find one item I liked enough to buy! That's never been a problem for me in this store ever before.

"How could this be?" I squealed to a saleslady who was the only available help around.

She validated my perception that this company had made decisions that compromised their core creed and culture in an effort to sell more goods to more people. As a result of its conscious dilution of merchandise and service functions, this special place that used to provide a unique shopping experience, especially for a department store, now looked and felt like every other department store.

Didn't the "powers that be" know what they were *really* selling? Sure, they were selling shoes, underwear, jewelry, blouses and skirts, but what were they *really* selling? My former favorite shopping venue had provided customers with service excellence and indulgent importance . . . that's what they were really selling! This became compromised when they abandoned their competitive edge, thus blending in with everyone else. Now my favorite "shopping event" was nothing more than a benign, flat-line experience.

In our businesses we *must* know who we are as a company, how we are different from our competition and why our customers buy from us. What is the underlying need our company can satisfy better than anyone else? Studying the competition is important, but it can be dangerous if you let it threaten your

" Where are the holes in how others do business that you can fill with innovation and service?"

originality. Sure, it's good to know what others in your industry are doing, and some say imitation is the greatest form of flattery. Personally, I find imitation to be an annoying coward's way of doing business. The *real* advantage of knowing what your competitors are doing is being able to identify where the "open spaces" are: Where are the holes in how others do business that you can fill with innovation and service? Show up there, where you can surprise your customers, treat your customers and indulgently serve your customers. Create your own edge and let others in your industry follow you.

# My life is my message.

GANDHI

SERVES YOU RIGHT!

# The Name Game

## Mixed Messages Keep Customers from Knowing Who You Are

It was at least a six-hour drive across the desert to the oceans of San Diego, and I welcomed the quiet emptiness of the time spent driving. I deciphered license plates, checked out truck and van logos, and imagined what other people's worlds were like.

One trailer in particular confused me. The company's name was Wildwood, yet the logo was a collection of blue ocean waves. Huh? The name Wildwood to me conjured up a lush forest with trees that touched the sky, and the simple graphic lines depicting cresting waves didn't match my picture at all.

In comparison, I remember to this day the Cheap Furniture booth I saw at a long-ago trade show. Unpainted tables and bookcases were displayed among brand-new copper pennies piled on the floor, on the tabletops, everywhere. How simple and direct can a message be? They literally were right on the money!

Does your company name serve your customer? Does your logo tell your company story with a picture? Does your customer have to work to figure you out? We know, as consumers ourselves, that if it takes longer than a New York minute to connect to and/or get the information we want/need, we're outta there!

I had a reality check about three months after I opened my doors, when a customer wandered into our Victorian Parlor. Sure, the oven and cookie counter sat center stage, and our name alone, Cookies from Home, clearly stated what our service was. Yet this customer saw only the old-fashioned armchairs and loveseat up against the lacy lattice windows, the old-time photographs on the wood-planked walls and the real *Life* magazines covering the beveled-glass coffee table. You got it: She thought we were selling antiques and collectibles! That was more than 20 years ago, and I'm grateful to her even today for teaching me an important lesson: What message am I sending to my customer, and am I serving my customer with a message that is consistent?

The language we use also should mindfully serve the positive perception of the customer's experience. I met a homebuilder at a recent business meeting who was passionate about his work. What confused me were his continual references to his many new "products" in the marketplace and how excited he was about building so many "units" that appeal to a certain niche of buyer. Never did I hear him use the words homes or housing, words that certainly would have engaged me in his vision so much more!

His language, you see, was an echo that recalled the very same lesson I learned back in the years when most

> "We know ... that if it takes longer than a New York minute to connect to and/or get the information we want/need, we're outta there!"

of my time was spent knocking on a lotta, lotta doors presenting my "product" to many corporate buyers. I had gotten caught up in big-shot business jargon. During the one appointment I still remember, my prospect patiently listened to my whole pitch and then leaned forward in his chair and softly asked me why I kept calling my cookies "product."

"Cookies sure sound a whole lot better to me," he said.

Oh, my, was he ever right!

If your company name, logo, language and merchandising are in line with your service, your customers have a much better chance of knowing exactly what you do and how they benefit from doing business with you. If the interpretation of your message is clear, direct and consistent, what a great message that is about how you run your business!

# It is obvious that the purpose of this world is not "to have and to hold" but "to give and serve."

SIR WILFRED GRENFELL

# Rethinking the "Nickel Tour"

## *Customers' Viewpoint Can Be Eye Opener*

We are all creatures of routine. We drive to work the same route every day. We arrive at our desks and routinely turn on the lights, music, computers . . . all signals to our mind and body that we're "open" and ready to do business. We go about our day, doing what we do, just as we've done every day before.

I liked my routine. I felt comfortable in my work environment. In fact, I often offered the "nickel tour" of our offices, kitchen and warehouse to colleagues and vendors who stopped by or had scheduled appointments, feeling proud of the now 21-year-old company that first started in my home kitchen. I'd walk visitors through our 12,000-square-foot facility, introducing them to staff in the various departments, acknowledging that the entrepreneurial spirit was alive and well in the personality of each workspace.

I probably still would be in that routine if it hadn't been for a friendly colleague who, while I was giving her the usual facility tour, remained quiet and unresponsive. When the nickel tour ended back in my office, she closed my door before she sat down to speak her mind. She said she would try to be gentle, but truly it was more important that she be direct.

What she saw on the tour were things I saw every day but didn't *really* see. She described a hodgepodge of furnishings; files and books stacked in every corner; cabinets and shelving in all sizes and colors; broken chairs and equipment lingering among their functioning replacements; gasping-for-life plants; and personalized clutter and memorabilia in every corner of every work station. Yes, our facility sure was clean, but this work environment was congested and neglected . . . and she knew this was not in alignment with my vision, philosophy and leadership creed.

What a wake-up call! I could hardly breathe as my heart began to pound. I bounced back and forth between anger at myself for my blind-sightedness and embarrassment for my staff and customers, to whom I had become numb and blind. As absolution, I hope this writing will be your wake-up call, too!

Today, right now, get over to the other side of your desk, to the other side of your sales counter. Walk in your front door and see what your customer sees. Stand there for a long time with a fresh viewpoint that looks for clean, attractive, nurtured surroundings . . . current pictures and magazines . . . clutter-free work areas . . .

"Once you can see you through your customers' eyes, you will be ready to provide the service that brought these customers to you in the first place."

comfortable, refurbished furniture . . . appropriate lighting . . . operating, functional equipment.

Once you can see you through your customers' eyes, you will be ready to provide the service that brought these customers to you in the first place. Before you can enter into any conversation or relationship with your customer—before you've even uttered one word—you have to hear what your work environment is saying.

I know, I know. This economy forces budget cuts and bare-bones spending. But it's amazing what a bucket of paint can do, along with increased mindful consciousness and effort among all team players.

Oh, and by the way, I proudly invite you to stop by my business. I would welcome the opportunity to give you what is now the "dollar" tour of our refurbished facility . . . and I'd welcome the chance to see it again and again through your eyes!

# The miracle is this:
# The more we give, the more we have.

LEONARD NIMOY

SERVES YOU RIGHT!

# You Lost Me at Hello!

*Greeter Sets Tone in Person
or on Phone*

A well-known, highly acclaimed restaurant missed the mark of 100 percent perfection after a very important but poorly made hiring decision—a decision that could cost the establishment more than management realizes. Managers mindfully and outstandingly addressed a unique ambiance, a creative and abundant menu, and over-the-top servers and busboys—but made a big mistake when they hired the wrong person to be their customers' first and most important human contact. The establishment's hostess is a sleepwalker, pale in comparison to the high-spirited energy that oozes from every other facet of this popular eatery. How could management overlook this necessary ingredient?

We arrived on time for our Saturday night reservation. While our heads bobbed right and left, eyes darting from the waterfall fixtures to the artistic and ample plates passing by, the hostess looked at us blankly and said she wouldn't seat us until the rest of our party arrived. We asked to be seated anyway, knowing our friends had just found a parking space a few blocks away. The hostess then said the real reason we couldn't be seated was because our table wasn't ready. Well, why didn't she say that in the first place? If she had simply explained that this was such a fun and terrific eating experience that customers tended to stay longer than expected, we would have understood and waited with even greater anticipation for what would soon be our turn.

For the next 20 minutes, I watched our hostess turn away and/or turn off customer after customer using one-word answers or curt one-liners to tell walk-ins it would be close to two hours before they could be seated. That might have been true, but surely there was a better way to deliver the message!

Every success-seeking business (and what business isn't?), whether it's a restaurant, a law office or a widget factory, must recognize the importance of its front-line connection with the customer. The person who answers the phone, the receptionist, the hostess or the sales clerk sets the tone for what often is the first and last impression your customers will experience.

Booker T. Washington offered the best wake-up call advice: "Excellence is doing a common thing in an uncommon way."

Try being your customer the next time you phone your office. Can your greeting be more upbeat or more personable? Does your company greeting stand out among all the other calls you've made that day? Do you see the opportunity here?

When you go to your office today, stop for a moment to see what your customer sees. Is there a smiling

"Every success-seeking business ... must recognize the importance of its front-line connection with the customer."

SERVES YOU RIGHT!

face to greet you? Is the person able to truly welcome your customers in a friendly, genuine way? Does the person know how important he or she is to your company and to you?

Knowing all the mindful decisions that must be made to make any business successful, it's easy—but inexcusable—to overlook the employee who is your customer greeter, whether in person or on the phone. Awareness is the first step. Notice the places you go, especially those that have made you their "raving fan." What's different? What makes you feel special and/or important? How can you apply the same tactic to your own company?

Here's your chance to raise your level of service from the ordinary "Hello, ABC Company. How can I direct your call?" to a *wow* greeting that is uniquely yours; one that lets your prospects and customers know they are important to you and you can hardly wait to serve them right!

# Don't give up when you still have something to give.

KOBI YAMADA

# Physician Heal Thyself

# Next!

## *Infusion of Caring Needed to Revive Medical Providers*

Why do they call doctor's appointments "doctor visits" when they're not visits at all? Why is the x-ray department now called the Imaging Center, when you're not exactly going in for a makeover? Seeing a doctor or having medical tests of any kind, even for routine annual checkups, always brings you face-to-face with your mortality and the "what ifs" you try so hard not to think about.

I had a certain amount of "what if" anxiety when I showed up at an Imaging Center for a routine exam and x-ray. Sign-in sheets greeted me. Women dressed in color-coordinated smocks that matched their office chairs walked through the office with expressionless faces, moving people (cattle?) in and out, here and there. It was like watching automated traffic control.

I was moved to the computer check-in area to be sure my insurance coverage was intact, even if all I needed was a Band-aid. I sat patiently, watching the clerk watch her computer. Once the paperwork was generated, she assertively placed the form and a pen in front of me with explicitly brief instructions to "sign here and here, and date it." She never looked at me or used my name.

She moved me to the next stop, where I sat in a row of hard, uncomfortable chairs with nothing to look at but dated and very used magazines. No music was playing, but I was treated to the background drone of afternoon soaps on a nearby TV. Every 20 minutes or so, a smocked "soldier" appeared to announce the last name of the next patient, sounding more like a sum-mons and sentencing than a welcome greeting.

When my name was called, I followed the nurse down a long, narrow corridor into a small, closet-like room. I waited and waited. A nurse with blank eyes came in, focused on the routine tasks of taking my blood pressure, temperature, height and weight, then noting these private observations on my history sheet. When the doctor finally came in for our "visit," she chatted with me for a few brief moments as the exami-nation was brought to a conclusion. I gathered my things and headed to the checkout counter. I wrote my check, said good-bye to the top of the bowed head of someone who never looked up to bid me farewell, and I was out the door.

Once outside, I breathed in fresh air and felt the sun heat my body. I took in one very long, deep breath, grateful to be alive and in good health.

How could a medical office be so sterile and human-less? Doctor's offices and treatment centers are in the business of treating humans. Servicing customers

> "Aliveness, humanness and compassion often are sorely lacking in the medical arena, where great customer service is needed most of all!"

(patients) with eye contact, name recognition, environmental warmth and some level of connection shouldn't be that difficult. In fact, it should be a top priority!

Yet it still amazes—and disappoints—me to see that aliveness, humanness and compassion often are sorely lacking in the medical arena, where great customer service is needed most of all! Why do men and women choose this line of work if they don't like people or see the importance of the human connection in healing? Can changes in health and managed care be blamed and held accountable for this pervasive condition?

The provocative film *Patch Adams* presented the same message, and the fact that it's a true story based on a real Patch Adams gives me hope. When someone looks at you and really sees you, when they say your name other than announcing "you're next," only then will you know you're in a place where you can trust the process of being cared for and healed . . . only then will they truly serve you right!

# People change and forget
# to tell each other.

LILLIAN HELLMAN

# First Impressions

## *Customers Won or Lost in Just Seven Seconds*

Networking 101 says you only get seven seconds to make a first impression. Those same seven seconds hold true when someone first walks into the reception area of your office. Too many times I see age-old magazines, well-worn seat cushions and thirsty plants.

Even worse than a tired ambiance is a greeter who considers the customer to be an intrusion to his or her administrative tasks or, worse still, an interruption of a personal conversation with a co-worker. Before one word is spoken, these other agendas are screaming messages, immediately putting your company behind the eight ball with an obvious disadvantage.

If someone walking into a medical office is greeted this way, quadrupled efforts will be needed to regain the "trust factor" because, in all likelihood, this neglect, apathy and boredom will be projected directly onto the concern and care the customer/patient anticipates receiving from the office and also the doctor.

Let me be specific. My internist informed me that, because of my age (don't ask!), it would be advisable for me to have several routine tests and procedures "just to be sure." She rattled off the names of several specialist doctors I could call when I was ready. I stalled as long as I could, but finally that "good girl following directions that were for my own good" syndrome took over.

Last on my list was a routine exam that involved one day for an outpatient procedure and recovery from anesthesia. Pulling my courage and humility from my toes, I called the office of a doctor on my internist's list to set up a consultation. I was surprised that a consultation with the doctor before the procedure was optional. Optional? That should have been my first clue that this doctor knocked out these procedures like a day full of teeth cleanings! Although I stayed in my "good girl" role, following directions and setting a procedural date, I realized by the end of this initial conversation that even if the doctor didn't want to see me before the surgery, I wanted to see her.

I was told to arrive a few minutes early on the day of my consultation to fill out paperwork. I was greeted by a view of the top of the receptionist's head as she pushed a clipboard into my hands and slid the glass window shut. This should have been my second clue.

Dutifully, I filled in the forms and returned my clipboard to the counter near the tightly shut window. I then walked back to my stiff, unyielding chair, where I sat for more than 35 minutes, looking at a small offering of reading material that included medical trade journals and two very old *Good Housekeeping* and

"Even worse than a tired ambiance is a greeter who considers the customer to be an intrusion to his or her administrative tasks."

*Parenting* magazines. This lackluster waiting (and more waiting) room should have been my third clue!

By the time I finally met the doctor, I was bored, angry and in high anxiety. When I was coldly ushered into an examination room instead of her office for a consultation appointment, and when my questions and her answers were not in sync, that did it. I couldn't wait to get out of there and, yes, I cancelled my procedural date with this doctor the very next day.

Clues are everywhere. The warmth and comfort of those first seven seconds when your customer enters your "space" sets the stage for your relationship, present and future. Why not get out from behind your desk *right now* and walk through your front door. What do you see? What do you feel? Are your front-line greeters enrolled and empowered with the importance of their job? Would *you* want to do business with *you*?

Why not let your open doors welcome your customers to a good feeling, a warm and friendly experience? In our world today, and specifically in this economy, service enthusiasm is indeed the greatest gift we can give each other.

# We cannot become what we need to be by remaining what we are.

MAX DEPREE

# Wimps Unite

*Stand Strong in Favor of
Healers with Heart*

I admit it. I'm a wimp. Usually my anticipation of
physical pain is a whole lot worse than the real thing,
like when I have to get flu shots or routine blood tests.
I know all about the "power of the mind" thing, but
my active imagination is easily stimulated, and that's
not always a good thing.

I had what I thought would be a no-brainer kind
of appointment with a dermatologist who was going to
look at and probably remove a few annoying bumps
that co-mingled with the freckles on my face. My only
experience of the receptionist was hearing her mono-
tone, inexpressive voice. She answered phones, scheduled appointments, confirmed co-pays with insurance
carriers and gave new patients forms to fill out, all at
the same time. A smile would have been nice, but, hey,
this lady had enough to do.

When my name was called, I walked into the small examining room and sat on the side chair rather than the patient's table. Relax, breathe and stay calm, I told myself. This is a no-brainer.

The doctor walked into the office a few minutes later, looking like the Man from Glad with a third eye. Wrapped in a clear cellophane jacket over scrubs, with a huge magnifying glass on his forehead, he beckoned me to sit on the edge of the table so he could give my bumps a closer look. I felt his breath on my face as he pressed and picked, all the while making grumbling noises.

With one hand on my shoulder, he reached with the other hand to open the door and call in his nurse. What was that about? Why was he calling in the nurse, I started to wonder. The wimp in me now sat up a little taller.

"What happens next?" I asked, trying to be casual.

He told me two of the three bumps just needed to be "scraped" and "burned." The third looked a "little suspicious," and he would need to do a different "procedure" on that one, he explained as the nurse handed me a sheet outlining "after-surgical care" for my wound.

"What?" I shrieked.

Scraped and burned? Suspicious? Procedure? The wimp in me was out in all her glory now, reacting to the language and pictures pounding on my brain's movie screen, not to mention the life-and-death possibilities that now seemed imminent.

"Hold on! Wait just a minute here! Can we talk?" I begged, tears of fear streaming down my soon-to-be-ravaged face.

He paused, stepped back and lifted the third eye at the top of his head. He looked at me for what I thought was really the first time. Although he was truly surprised at my overreaction (duh!), he realized his approach could have been a bit more human.

"Wouldn't it be just too terrific if care, concern and compassion filled those moments when mortality issues remind you that life is short?"

SERVES YOU RIGHT!

He answered my questions, explained the procedure, promised to communicate the results to me sooner than "seven to ten days," and tried, from that point on, to soften his language and be gentler with his information.

Now don't get me wrong. I want to know what I need to know. But wouldn't it be just too terrific if care, concern and compassion filled those moments when mortality issues remind you that life is short?

I know, I know. It's all because of managed care. It's all because of the squeeze that forces doctors to work harder for less money. I know all that. But we wimps out there need more than what we're getting. Doctors' offices should be sanctuaries staffed with people who know how important their jobs are, people who care about the human spirit as well as the human body. For this one and only body of mine, I sure would appreciate a little bit of humanness, a little bit of handholding once in a while.

There are healers who know how to give. There are healers who truly and sensitively want to give. Why should we settle for less?

# When I give, I give myself.

WALT WHITMAN

# Dr. Welby Lives . . .

## But Caring Healers
## Becoming Sweet Memory

Dr. Marcus Welby is alive and well. In fact, he's still practicing medicine and making house calls in Phoenix, Arizona.

For those of you who don't remember the television hero of the '70s, Dr. Welby was the family doctor who delivered babies, helped children survive chicken pox and measles, guided teenagers through acne and puberty, and treated adults for strep throat, stomach flu and other ailments encountered through life's passages. Along with *Ozzie & Harriet* and *Father Knows Best,* Dr. Welby is a flash from the long ago past, when we still believed in heroes and happy endings. Ah, those were the days . . .

Dr. James Dearing, a surgeon and physician of family medicine, called after reading a column in which I pleaded for more humane service from most of today's insensitive doctors. Dr. Dearing invited me to witness the other side of the equation by experiencing the routines and challenges facing a family doctor who cares for patients ranging in age from one day to 104 years old. Invitations like that don't cross my path very often, and I admit I was intrigued beyond curiosity. I certainly knew how it felt to be the patient: a number, a file, a hunk of flesh that required a look-see or perhaps a test, and a quick diagnosis that moved me out the door fast. My name, my history and my fears were rarely asked for or needed.

I took Dr. Dearing up on his offer, and a few days later I entered a quiet courtyard looking for suite number 1. Suites 3 and 4 screamed for recognition, with lists of the many services provided within printed in white letters on black glass. Suite 1 was almost invisible except for a barely legible brass plate that told the doctor's name and type of practice. Upon entering, I felt comfortable in a well-worn reception area that was loaded with current magazines for all ages and interests. As I was ushered into Dr. Dearing's office, I noticed wall-to-wall files, folders and stacks of reports begging for attention.

Dr. Dearing is Dr. Welby. He is a healer with heart. He cares for and nurtures the relationships he shares with his patients and their families. Nothing else could explain why he does all he does—and this man does a lot! He has a full-fledged family practice (though he confesses he doesn't deliver babies anymore), he teaches, he serves on several boards, he's the "team doc" at the local high school, and he still manages to be ever-present with his wife and family. He reads everything he needs to read about medicine, and he reads what his patients read so he can better understand their lives. I watched him dance among his patients, who want just one more minute of his time; his students, to whom he gives more questions than answers; the pharmaceutical reps, who woo him in the hallways; and his staff of seven, who look to him for direction and process.

He laughs with, hugs and interacts with his patients in a comfortable, relaxed manner. He knows their names and the names of their husbands, wives or mothers. He listens to them, hearing what they say and what they don't say.

**"I watched him dance among his patients ..."**

Take, for example, the woman who was there because of her aching shoulder. After asking several questions about her symptoms and validating her discomfort, he asked me to leave the room so he could talk to her privately. Indeed, she was under considerable stress and strain from some personal problems that recently had surfaced in her life.

"Pain may show up in the body, but often it shows up in the mind first," Dr. Dearing later explained.

How easy it would have been to simply give this lady a pain pill and send her on her way!

Then there was a male patient who had some ear problems from flying so much recently. Sure, Dr. Dearing wanted to solve the problem, but he also asked where the patient had been traveling so he could relate more to the patient and his experience.

"It's all about relationship," he said. "Why else would I be here?"

Indeed, that is the million-dollar question. With today's managed care and the high cost of malpractice insurance, coupled with "doctor hoppers" who flit from one doctor to the next, sometimes not even paying their minimal co-pays, it's no wonder the good docs get worn down. Expectations are not met for either side because of these random rather than historical relationships.

The doctor's workload is doubled, and there's a tremendous cost to process all the paperwork for lab tests, follow-up procedures, callbacks and prescription refills. Make no mistake; none of this work generates income. Doctors are choosing to quit medicine altogether, to operate independently outside the system, or to stay in this game and "process patients" without relationship priority and sensitivity.

Swell. Where does this leave you and me? Does this mean we just surrender to less service, less care? Do we allow the few Dr. Dearing's left out there to fade into the sunset as a sweet memory? How will we ever survive a system that is killing our spirit . . . and our caring healers?

# The willingness to create a new vision is a statement of your belief in your potential.

DAVID MCNALLY

# Finding Doctor Right!

## *Priority Assessment is Key When Choosing Doctor*

Have you ever been fired by your doctor? Well, neither had I until I asked for more customer service than my doctor was willing to provide. I worried I would be treated like Elaine on *Seinfeld* when no doctor would accept her as a patient because one doctor had written in her medical file that she was "difficult." Would that now be my fate because of a clash of wills, a clash of opinions on customer service issues?

I was unprepared. I hadn't checked on prescription expiration dates, routine exam dates and, most importantly, a backup plan for my medical care. I needed a plan, and I needed it now. I had been given a terrific opportunity to find my Doctor Right if only I could stop my paranoia and hyperventilating! Somewhere in the world of medical nirvana, there was a doctor who could hardly wait to serve me right. First, however, I had to identify what was important to me in this relationship, because without my health and well being nothing else matters, right? So, I blessed my previous doctor and thanked her for reminding me that, yes, I do have a choice.

My list of questions became the framework for my search. Assessing medical expertise was my first priority. After that, my focus centered on values and attitudes. What was the doctor's medical philosophy and what role did he/she take with patients? How accessible was the doctor and what customer service policies and procedures did he/she follow? Did I want a single doctor's office or a large group of physicians? Was I more comfortable with a scientist or a free thinker who considered alternative methods of healing? What were my needs at this time of my life? How human was the office staff? Was the office environment thoughtful of my comfort? Was the doctor interested in my feelings as well as my physical condition? Was this a doctor who listened, really listened, to my needs and concerns?

Armed with the right questions, I decided to accept this mission. I talked about doctors everywhere I went. I asked friends, colleagues, other doctors, hairdressers, personal trainers, manicurists, business contacts. I started to hear many of the same names and was able to identify five doctors to interview.

My next step was to set an appointment that wasn't an examination. One office dismissed me immediately, saying the doctor "simply doesn't have that kind of time." That response gave me my answer, and now I was down to four. The next office I called agreed to an appointment, but the doctor was so busy I'd have to wait four months.

With three doctors remaining, I was surprised when I discovered the next doctor already had a "meet and greet" policy in place for new patients. When I walked into his office ten days later, I felt comfortable in the small, cheerful reception area. A smiling, friendly person greeted me, and I recognized her voice as the same person who had given me directions when she confirmed my appointment the day before. My customer service heart began to skip a beat. I had heard from a friend that this doctor called her personally one Friday afternoon to let her know that her test results gave her a clean bill of health. He didn't want her to worry needlessly over the weekend. This was my kind of doctor! We spent 20 minutes together, and he willingly shared his philosophy about seeing himself as a teacher who does his best to think like his patients. Music to my ears!

My second call was to a doctor whose office staff wasn't quite sure what to do with my request for an interview. The next day, I received a call to schedule an appointment. Three weeks later, a machine confirmed my appointment for the next day. This was a very busy office. When the receptionist insisted I fill out new patient forms, even though I explained I wasn't sure if I was a new patient, I finally surrendered because it was easier to fill them out than to upset her system.

I waited for the doctor in her office. Every inch of space was taken up with children's drawings, photographs, plants, books, files and memorabilia. In she walked, larger than life with her robust energy and personable presence. Within minutes, I heard laughter—indeed a rare occurrence in a doctor's office—as she shared her philosophy on life and healing. I felt my shoulders relax, my breath deepen and my stomach stop gurgling. This was a very human being.

"Somewhere in the world of medical nirvana, there was a doctor who could hardly wait to serve me right."

I had to wait more than two months to meet the third doctor. A young voice had confirmed my appointment the day before in a message on my voice mail. Because I had to wait awhile for this meeting, I expected the hustle and bustle of a busy office, and I was surprised when I entered a very calm, soothing and rather intimate reception area. Dark walls, soft lighting and comfy seating relaxed me.

When I was brought into the doctor's office, she was there to greet me. She was a gentlewoman, mirroring her calm, serene surroundings. A large Buddha sat behind her, somewhat camouflaged by abundant greenery all around. She was soft-spoken, yet very direct in sharing her opinions and concerns, especially on the important issue of personal choice and empowerment. She was quite vocal about managed care, medical laws and the loss of her own freedom as a physician. Yes, we talked healing philosophies and office policies, but our conversation went much deeper than that. She validated my search for Doctor Right, and when I left her office I felt inspired and dedicated to the pursuit of exploration.

So who was the winner? Who was the lucky doctor who won me as a new patient? Truthfully, I could have selected any one of these three physicians, and isn't that great news? There is hope and no reason to settle for less! We do get to choose, though sometimes we forget that until we move to a new city or decide to seek a new level of relationship with our primary care physicians.

Healing, just like every other business, is about relationship. Because we live longer and hopefully healthier lives, we are responsible for choosing doctors who are aligned with our personal vision and totally committed to doing whatever it takes to make us feel whole in every way.

# Service Is a
# Two-Way Street

# It Takes Two

*Want Service? Speak Up*

Getting great customer service is not a psychic phenomenon: Servers and sellers in the marketplace are not mind readers! They don't know your situation, expectations or individual preferences for the moment, and unless you communicate your desires it just ain't gonna happen. You, the consumer, need to participate by doing more than just showing up.

I'm sure I've made many a restaurant server uneasy while trying to communicate non-verbally what it would take to make me happy: staring longingly at a cushy booth across the room when I was sitting on a stiff, unyielding chair . . . looking at my watch every two minutes because I was in a hurry and wondering why I couldn't get served faster . . . allowing my plate to be removed before I was done eating, when I was just resting between bites . . . or shouting across the table to my companion because the music was too loud to have a conversation. Not once, even in the height of frustration, did I look my server in the eye and request what I wanted.

"Enough!" I reminded myself. "I *must* speak my mind and let them know what I want." Maybe, just maybe, I can then have a positive dining experience in a restaurant.

"I know directly asking for what you want isn't always easy, but if you don't speak up you can't expect the other person to read your mind."

So I put myself to the test. I asked a male colleague to join me for a business lunch at a popular local restaurant. After the hostess greeted us, she directed us toward a dark, desolate corner of the room that would have been ideal if romance was the focus, but this was business as usual. I kindly asked her if we could sit in a brighter part of the restaurant near the big picture window, where we could watch airplanes come and go. As she pointed to a table in the middle of the open area, I asked her, kindly once again, if we could sit in the periphery of this space because we would be talking business and needed more privacy than the center of the room allowed. She remained amicable and most willing to accommodate my requests. We were on the brink of great customer service here, and we achieved a win/win solution. I communicated my preferences. She listened and then made it happen—simple as that.

I believe most businesses really do intend to serve the customer right. I believe most businesses do want to model themselves after exemplary role models like Nordstrom and The Ritz Carlton. I believe most businesses do "talk the talk" in training their employees and reinforcing the "customer is king" creed. So why is it a rare event to actually experience the ultimate in customer service?

The simple explanation is that it takes two to make it happen. Think about the last time you had an unpleasant customer service experience, which was probably recently. Did you share your vision with the person serving you, whether it was about where you wanted to sit in a restaurant, how deep you wanted your body massage or what kind of insurance you thought you needed to buy?

I know directly asking for what you want isn't always easy, but if you don't speak up you can't expect the other person to read your mind. It's a set-up, doomed to disappointment and frustration. And you know what? It serves you right!

# We are all here on earth to help others; what on earth the others are here for, I don't know.

W. H. AUDEN

# Pushy! Pushy!

## *As the Customer, You're in Charge*

Shopping can be serious business. You need to concentrate and stay focused. You want the freedom to look and choose. When you need information or service, it should be at your request, right? Right! After all, you're the customer, and without you a store doesn't exist. So what do you do when your salesperson turns into a pit bull? What do you do when the balance of power appears to have shifted to the other side?

A friend recently told me in not-so-gentle terms that my hiking wardrobe, no matter how great I accessorized, just didn't fit in on the trails. Off I went to my neighborhood hiking and camping stores with my budget set and checkbook in hand.

In the first store, I occasionally spotted a salesperson, but most of the time I was left to fend for myself. It's a jungle out there, but I managed to find most of the basics for my new "happy trails" look. In the next store, I faced a more life-threatening situation when a saleslady pounced on me as soon as my left foot crossed the threshold. I was her reason for being! She hovered over me like a lioness keeping her cub on a very short leash, wanting to please me, I'm sure. I soon had more clothes in my dressing room than I have in my entire closet. Besides hiking clothes, she brought me summer dresses, shirts, jackets, even summer sleepwear. She insisted each was a "must have." I kept showing her my list of the few items I still needed, but she obviously had a different agenda. She was committed to selling me, not serving me.

Then I remembered: Hey! I'm the customer! I'm the one in control here! The purpose of this store—no, every store—is to entice me to spend my money. The displays and merchandise, the store design, the staff training, the market research and advertising, the shopping ambiance—*everything* is geared to making me a happy camper, right? Right!

To regain your position of strength, try these strategies:

**Inform the salesperson what would make you comfortable.** Do you want to be left alone? Do you want an occasional check-in? Do you want your salesperson close at hand and ever-present? There is no right or wrong answer . . . only what's best for you and your comfort level.

**Move up the ranks if your needs aren't met.** If you've communicated your desires and the salesperson has not accommodated you, ask for the supervisor and request another salesperson to assist you. Again, define your terms, your boundaries and your needs.

**Shop elsewhere if still not satisfied.** If even this fails and you're not being heard, simply leave the store.

> "I kept showing her my list of the few items I still needed, but she obviously had a different agenda. She was committed to selling me, not serving me."

Remember you, as the customer, have that power. There are *very* few items that can be bought only in that store, and unless you're getting the service and attention you deserve, why pay for a miserable shopping experience?

**Take it to the top.** In most cases, the owners or corporate officers would be most unhappy to know such a situation occurred in their store. They would greatly appreciate a letter from you, explaining how or why they failed to make—and keep—you as a satisfied customer. If you don't tell them, nothing will change. Don't just disappear with your anger and frustration; give them a chance to make it right with you. They need and want to know how to serve you better.

# If people believe in the company they work for, they pour their heart into making it better.

HOWARD SCHULTZ

SERVES YOU RIGHT!

# Disarming a Snooty Salesperson

## *Service Is a Two-Way Street*

When you are the customer, how do you keep your ego and temper in check when you shop at a high-end store and come face-to-face with "snooty" salespeople? You can see it when they look at you or, even worse, when they don't. In their eyes, you appear to be either a waste of time or an invisible entity.

We've all been there! A lady friend of mine, who is a successful physician, left her garden in a hurry one Saturday afternoon when she remembered she needed a hat for the next day's golf tournament. She didn't want just any old hat. She wanted to make a statement with a hat she had seen the week before at a fine boutique in the mall.

When she walked into the store wearing rather plain shorts and a T-shirt, with dirt from her garden still under her unmanicured nails, the salesperson barely greeted her. My friend pointed to the $250 bonnet on the top shelf and asked the salesperson for a closer look. That's when "20 Questions" began, as the salesperson attempted to qualify or, more likely, disqualify the customer.

My friend is known for her eccentric style and sense of humor, and I'm sure she was utterly enjoying the interrogation, giving answers that only infuriated, confused and frustrated the salesperson. My friend paid cash for her stylized hat, knowing she would now be the center of attention on the golf course the next day. The salesperson was most surprised to see several $100 bills grace her sales counter from what appeared to be a most unlikely source.

Ah! That old adage about judging a book by its cover . . . and so it goes.

How do you neutralize a "snooty" sales encounter? By stating your objective, establishing your credibility and validating your adversary. Let's apply these concepts to the above scenario:

**State your objective.** By communicating your objective, you encourage the salesperson's enrollment and increase the likelihood of a positive interaction. My physician friend, for example, could have said, "If you have time, I'm looking to purchase a hat in a $200 price range, and I'm somewhat in a hurry." Had she done this, the salesperson would have known immediately that she meant business.

**Establish your credibility.** While my friend was stating her objective to the salesperson, she could have simultaneously taken $250 in cash out of her wallet or flashed her platinum or gold credit card to indicate to

> "I'm sure she was utterly enjoying the interrogation, giving answers that only infuriated, confused and frustrated the salesperson."

the salesperson she was obviously a qualified and credible buyer.

**Validate your adversary.** If you approach a salesperson to do your bidding, you are creating an adversary. However, if you validate a salesperson as a problem solver who can help you get what you want, you have created a partner. Obviously, my friend did not meet the salesperson half way when questioned about her possible purchase. A frustrating game of "20 Questions" could have been prevented had my friend validated the salesperson by saying, "I really want to make an impact at this golf tournament, and I need your help finding the perfect hat. Your store has always had such beautiful hats, and I know you can help me!" Most likely, this type of validation will come as such a shock that the salesperson's "attitude" will be replaced by a humanness you both will enjoy during the transaction.

Instead of being offended or intimidated the next time you come face-to-face with a "snooty" salesperson, try any one of these ideas in an effort to create a win/win solution. If you're successful, it will serve you right!

# Caring is a powerful business advantage.

SCOTT JOHNSON

# What's Wrong with This Picture?

*Ask for What You Deserve and Expect Company to Fulfill Promise*

Going to the movies can be an addictive escape. When problems are no longer embraced as opportunities and the stress of the day takes your breath away, there's something quite soothing about sitting in a dark theater watching someone else's life instead of thinking or worrying about your own.

For a much-needed vacation, what could be a better escape than a movie marathon ala the Telluride Film Festival? My husband and I had talked about going for years, but this was the year we were finally making it happen. Besides, we were so exhausted that the thought of doing anything more physical than feeding our faces with an unlimited supply of popcorn seemed like too much of a stretch for us.

Registering for the festival was no easy task. You had to secure a place to stay long before they issued your pass to the movies. Thousands of people crowd this little Colorado village for festivals, and we were told we should feel grateful to have a room at all!

When we finally found our assigned room within a maze of concrete, instead of the romantic hideaway we requested, we were so outraged that we lost our grip on socially approved behavior. They had set up a full-fledged temporary kitchen within *inches* of the singular window in our closet-like room. The noise of the staff, the constant humming of the ovens and the smells early in the morning, compounded by this claustrophobic cell, would never do; no way, no how.

I watched my husband, who is usually the calm one—my compassionate and mellow Renaissance man—turn purplish-red with rage. He was gritting his teeth inside clenched jaws and had a slight curl to his upper lip as he stomped out of our less-than-basic room and marched back to the reservation desk. I, for once, sat quietly in our cave, waiting, oh-so-patiently for my man to return with better news.

He was gone a very long time. Both the manager and assistant manager were at lunch when he first arrived at the front desk, which was a good thing because he had time to breathe and develop his plan of attack. While waiting, he found the perfect weapon: A framed poster within view inside the manager's office depicted a firm, tightly clutched handshake, the exact metaphor of what Barry wanted as a happy ending and resolution to our situation at hand (no pun intended!). He pointed to the picture several times during his engaging dialogue with the manager, reminding her that this was her moment of truth, her time to walk her talk.

Indeed she did. Although every room and bed were taken for the weekend, there was a two-bedroom, two-bath condo with a kitchenette and spa that was a last-minute cancellation, priced at more than triple what we had agreed to pay for our original basic motel room. That will do just fine, my Mighty Mouse husband declared, as he waited for her to confirm that, yes, this super deluxe condo was ours at our motel room price.

Thanks to his courage and willingness to enter into battle, our vacation budget was intact and our living quarters felt like we had won the lottery. After days and nights of watching films about other people's lives, we couldn't wait to get back to our own when it was all over.

So speak up! Ask for what you deserve. Look for clues in a company's philosophy and image, and be there to remind staff members to live up to the company promise. In most cases, you'll receive even more than you expect and not a bit less than you deserve.

# When people go to work, they look to you for heat as well as light.

---

WOODROW WILSON

# 'Tis the Season

## *Shopping Mania Shouldn't Wring Joy Out of Holidays*

Holiday shopping can be like guerilla warfare: elbows up as you plow through the crowds, making tracks across mall miles; putting your life on the line for a parking space; and spending scads more dollars than you should because the frenzy has convinced you you'll never get another chance if you don't buy now.

But wait a minute . . . just wait a minute. I love to give. I love to shop, especially at holiday time. It's my mission and purpose to hunt down the ultimate gift for each of my lucky recipients. I swoon when the smile in someone's eyes confirms that the gift I have chosen has, indeed, hit the mark. So how can I stay in the glow of giving? How can I create an attitude adjustment so I can still enjoy the process? Here are a few "service tips" that might help us all rejoice in the beauty and joy of the season of giving:

**Do your homework.** Write your list of gift ideas ahead of time, along with your budget and price range for each. I guarantee you'll save money if you are organized and focused. Also, consolidate your shopping logistics by identifying and purchasing more in fewer locations.

**"If they deserve your business, they will want to know how to serve you better. They will welcome your feedback."**

**Ask for what you need.** If you are not getting the level of sales assistance you need, don't settle for less. Communicate to managers, owners and/or corporate offices. If they deserve your business, they will want to know how to serve you better. They will welcome your feedback.

**Validate your adversary.** When your salesperson seems pressured, flustered, scattered, exhausted or all of the above, offer a little compassion, a little bit of gratitude. Holiday time is not an easy time, especially for retailers who work long hours and deal with customers who are not as nice as you. Your validation of them will go a long way toward gaining better service for yourself.

**Use buying power to your advantage.** Remember that businesses need you in order to stay in business. Rarely is what you need offered only in one store. If you are not being served and appreciated as a customer, spend your dollars somewhere else!

**Set your mental attitude.** Giving is truly a joy. Picture your loved ones appreciating your thoughtfulness. Smile more. Relax more. Be grateful. Enjoy. So what if it's crowded? So what if someone pulled into your parking space? Dress yourself with a bright, cheery smile and a Teflon back.

You'll see that these service tips, along with your holiday spirit, not only will bring you a joyous celebration, but also will serve you right!

# Sincere words of praise are absolutely free—and worth a fortune.

SAM WALTON

# Who's on First?

## *In-Store Customers Take Priority over Phones*

What happens when you are in the midst of a transaction in a store and the salesperson's phone rings? It's frustrating. It's rude. In fact, it's a downright insult.

You made the decision to get in your car and trek across town, combating traffic, heat and time to go directly to a chosen store. Your intention, most likely, was to get more information and probably make a purchase. There you are, patiently waiting your turn, until you finally have the salesperson's attention. You explain your situation and what you need, but in the middle of a sentence the phone rings at the counter where you're standing. For the first time, you notice a sign on the back wall that says, "Phone calls may interrupt sales transactions. Please be patient." Yeah, right!

It seems to me the customer who's standing there, live and in person, ready to buy, should take priority. If you're that customer, how can you handle the situation without losing your cool while getting what you need at the same time?

True, much depends on what kind of store you're in. If it's a pharmacy, the call could be an emergency and truly the right priority. If it's a department store, you have the option of going to another sales counter and starting all over again. But if it's a one-counter store, the call could be personal or business. If there's no one other than your salesperson to answer the phone, it is only right that you allow a reasonable amount of time—no more than a few minutes—for the person to put the telephone customer on hold or promise a call back. After all, your time is valuable, too. You might have people waiting in the car or maybe you've taken part of your lunch hour to handle this errand, and now it's time for you to get back to work.

If the salesperson does not acknowledge you in the appropriate timeframe, interrupt the phone conversation and remind him that you were in the middle of a conversation when the phone rang and you'd like to take priority and conclude this transaction. That should do it.

If it doesn't, take your salesperson's name and make sure he sees you doing just that. Announce that you will communicate with the owner or parent of the company about the situation and level of non-service you received. Then leave and take your business to the competition. Hopefully, they have studied and shopped other stores like theirs, and they know how to shine where their competition doesn't.

If you would rather win at their game—and, yes, I guess this is a rather spiteful solution—why not use your cell phone or a nearby pay phone to call and tell

"It seems to me the customer who's standing there, live and in person, ready to buy, should take priority."

the salesperson you're the same individual who was standing in front of him just moments ago? Or you could place a call to a competitor right there in the sales line. Perhaps then the salesperson would give you the attention you deserved in the first place. Perhaps then he would see the absurdity of the situation. Perhaps then he would understand the priority.

# Let no one come to you without leaving better.

MOTHER TERESA

SERVES YOU RIGHT!

# Sometimes Customers Are the Problem

*Salesperson or Shopper,*
*Courtesy Never Goes Out of Style*

Is the customer always right? Do we own some of the responsibility for creating good customer service?

Let's face it: Customer service is about relationship, and it takes two to tango. Yes, good service is a wonderful surprise, and astonishing service can take your breath away. But there are good—even great—employees out there, and sometimes the problem comes from a rude and abusive customer.

I know, I know. We're in denial that maybe, just maybe, our moods, problems and attitudes push the limits of the people who are trying to serve us.

Meet Mary, a 67-year-old woman who moved to Arizona from the Bronx. She left her family and all else that was familiar when she began her new life in Arizona. She lives with her two cats and works two jobs, one as a bookkeeper for a local interior design firm and the other as a salesperson of linens and fine china in a well-trafficked department store. She is gracious and genuine in her every effort to serve. Because of this intention, she has built a very loyal following of customers she stays in touch with regularly. She knows what her customers like, and when items come in or go on sale she gives them a jingle to let them know. After she spends time with a customer, she sends a thank-you note expressing her appreciation for their business. And here's the best part: Mary gets paid an hourly wage with no commission. She does her job because she loves to serve. Indeed, her customers love her for it.

Enter Ms. Smith, a woman in her late 40s, well-groomed and beautifully coifed. She was either in a hurry—a big hurry—or her basic nature was terribly impatient. She ignored the line of customers waiting to pay for their must-have purchases, and went right up to the register, tapping her fingernail on the counter to get Mary's attention. Mary maintained her composure and eye contact with her existing customer, but Ms. Smith persisted and finally interrupted Mary's conversation, telling her she had a return and didn't want to wait much longer to be taken care of. Mary stayed true to her unruffled nature while everyone watched Ms. Smith percolating with intensified momentum.

"Why are you so shorthanded? Where is your manager?" Ms. Smith asked rudely, tapping her nails and building toward stomping her feet.

True, these were legitimate questions, but the tone in her voice didn't indicate concern or compassion for Mary. Still, Mary kept her cool, asking the next customer if she minded an interruption while she handled the return. The next customer in line was almost as anxious to send Ms. Smith on her way as Mary was! Ms. Smith took her bag and emptied the return merchandise onto the counter. The receipt floated to the ground like a feather and landed on the floor between the women's feet. Everyone stood frozen in silence to see what would happen next. Who should bend down to retrieve that vital piece of paper: an irate customer or a 67-year-old saleslady who was doing her best to stay professional in a heated situation?

When Ms. Smith stood there defiantly, clinging to her "rights" as the customer, Mary finally drew the line. She moved closer to Ms. Smith, looked her right in the eye and calmly said, "Ms. Smith, perhaps you are confusing service with servitude. I think it would be best if I got the manager to help you."

The crowd that had gathered applauded Mary as she proudly walked to the back of her department, leaving the receipt pinned under Ms. Smith's big toe. Another salesperson might have collapsed or surrendered under the pressure to perform created by this rude, insensitive customer.

Was it a power struggle? Was it an ego problem for both parties? I used to believe the customer was always right, but I've learned that's not always true. Some customers are downright difficult and almost impossible to please. If you've ever been a salesperson, you know sometimes you can have the best intentions and the patience of a church full of saints, yet still have customers who take you to the edge.

Although this was a retail situation, there are other common courtesies we customers rarely extend to salespeople. Courtesies like calling ahead to cancel an appointment instead of just not showing up. Courtesies like telling the truth if we're not interested in buying

> "I used to believe the customer was always right, but I've learned that's not always true."

instead of not returning phone calls. Courtesies like being on time for appointments, recognizing the salesperson's time is as valuable as ours. Think about it.

Yes, I know good customer service is a rare event, rude is in and smiling is a sin because mediocrity is the norm. But what would it be like if we as customers extended a little compassion, a little appreciation and a little consideration once in awhile? Maybe, just maybe, customer service would improve. The more you give, the more you get. Catch salespeople doing something good and acknowledge them. They certainly won't expect the applause of gratitude, and I can bet you will get their appreciation in return.

# What a wonderful miracle, if only we could look through each other's eyes for an instant.

THOREAU

# Egypt or Bust!

*Trip of a Lifetime Gets Lost in Sand*

Egypt was never high on my travel wish list, but when my friend and I attended a spiritually powerful seminar, we were attracted to a table that ignited our desire to join the speaker on an Egyptian pilgrimage. The Tour Lady informed us only 200 people (only 200?) could go, and there were just a few spaces left. I should have recognized this deadline sales technique, but my heart, not my head, was in control at the moment. We signed up right then, knowing we had ten months to save our money and anticipate what we hoped would be a life-changing experience.

The day finally came. Like two schoolgirls, my friend and I giggled on the airplane in anticipation of the adventure that awaited us. After an incredibly long journey—22 hours to be exact—we arrived at our hotel and the first orientation meeting. The Tour Owners spent hours reviewing the dos and don'ts of Egypt, telling us what we could and couldn't do. They kept us on a pretty short leash, and I could see why as I looked around the jam-packed room. That's when Mrs. Tour Owner proudly announced they now had 478 people instead of 200!

With nearly 500 people, we're talking a week filled with cattle herding. Considerable time was spent waiting in line for cold breakfasts or Americanized buffet lunches consisting of flavorless Egyptian dishes that appealed to most tastes. Important communications were incomplete or nonexistent. For example, seeing the Sphinx at sunrise was a powerful event, but neither my friend nor I were dressed warmly enough because we hadn't been told that strong, cold winds blow across the desert at 4:30 in the morning. It was difficult to have a spiritual experience when you were frozen to the bone!

The next day we both had sore throats, and several days later my friend was so sick with a high fever she asked the Tour Owner to send a physician to our room. As a result, she was unable to attend an optional tour the next day. Not only did she not receive a phone call of concern to see how she was feeling, but it also took tremendous persistence and determination before she was finally able to get her $50 refund for the tour she missed. Mr. Tour Owner couldn't be bothered with such details—not when he was trying to control close to 500 people!

Early on, my friend wisely detached from the group and her expectations. Not me. I anticipated each day, each event. And each day I crashed with disappointment.

The day they provided a buffet lunch and invited an Egyptian band to play for us sounded like a nice touch of local color—until the Egyptians began playing their version of "Yankee Doodle Dandy"! Up to the last night, I continued to look for transformation. The itinerary promised a light show at the Sphinx and Pyramid, to be viewed from the rooftop of a private residence. How could that be anything less than spectacular? But have you ever tried putting 400 people on someone's roof? It was a sham. Besides feeling terribly sorry for myself, I was also embarrassed for Mrs. Tour Owner, who was obviously in over her head and not the least bit effective in trying to control the crowd.

There was no consideration for the customer on even the most obvious level, such as instructions for checking out. Some people had a second week on the tour (God help them) and some, like my friend and me, were flying out at 1:30 in the morning. Logistics are key in cattle herding, and it would have seemed appropriate to receive written communication regarding luggage, the day's itinerary and check out the night before our departure date. Instead, Mrs. Tour Owner announced all these rules and regulations at our morning feed, 20 minutes before we were scheduled to leave on the last day's tour. We rushed to our room, rushed to finish packing, rushed to check out and rushed to our tour bus, wondering what we had forgotten. This also meant we were homeless from 9:30 in the morning until we left for the airport at 9:30 that night, left with no private bathroom, no place to rest and no place to leave our most personal belongings. The 22-hour flight home was a welcome relief after this level of incompetence and inconsideration!

I've tried to forgive them—and myself—for the money lost, the unfulfilled dreams and the bitter disappointment in not having a single epiphany. I can only assume Mr. & Mrs. Tour Owner have learned about controlled growth and the consequences of greed. They didn't think like their customer. They didn't create

"It was difficult to have a spiritual experience when you were frozen to the bone!"

community or connection with their customer. They chose quantity versus quality. They ended the possibility of building a relationship so the customer would want to do business with them again and again. It seems they have a lot to learn about customer service.

However, part of the dreadful experience was my fault, too. As the customer, I needed to be more responsible. I needed to know my travel comfort level. I needed to do my homework, checking references and customer-service priorities. When these types of issues are in alignment—then and only then—can we enjoy the unforgettable experience we all dream of having when we travel.

# The greatest tragedy is indifference.

THE RED CROSS

# Meet Susan Brooks

Susan Brooks is, and always has been, a service enthusiast! Today many know her as the "Cookie Queen," but her passion for service started in the classroom, where her first customers were her high school English students. Teaching seven years and having a Master's degree in education, Susan created an inspiring curriculum that motivated and challenged her students.

Today, with more than 25 years as a business owner, Susan taps into these same talents and skills as she pursues excellence in both product and service, inspiring her staff to astonish and exceed customers' expectations. As the co-founder, president and visionary of Cookies From Home, her common sense approach to business and her intention to serve has transformed her dream into what is today a multimillion-dollar gift and mail order company. Service enthusiasm throughout every department at Cookies From Home is one of the driving forces that has made her company so successful.

Her achievements have been recognized by many publications, including *Town and Country, New Woman, Entrepreneurial Woman* and *Working Woman* magazines. Susan was a finalist in *Inc.'s* Entrepreneur of the Year Award, and her company was selected Small Business of the Year by the Tempe, Arizona, Chamber of Commerce. She was chosen as a regional finalist in the *Working Woman* Entrepreneurial Awards for customer service excellence and was recognized by the *Phoenix Business Journal* as one of the "Valley's influential leaders" in the city's business community. Most recently, she was a finalist for the Business in Excellence Award from the Tempe Chamber of Commerce, as well as having the prestigious honor of being chosen a Woman of Distinction by the Girl Scouts of Arizona.

Susan's "Serves You Right!®" column has successfully appeared in national publications and the *Arizona Republic*, and currently runs in the *Business Journal*. As a national speaker and trainer for the past nine years, Susan challenges her business and organizational audiences to renew their spirit and better serve their customers. She customizes every presentation to focus on the client's specific needs and objectives. Susan energizes her audience with interactive programs so they can have fun while they learn. She has spoken to audiences as large as 1,000 and as intimate as 25.

"My mission is to hold up a mirror as a wake-up call so businesspeople can see what the customer sees," Susan says. "Maybe, just maybe, I can help create a shift in customer service consciousness in the marketplace, helping to make this world a better place by giving customers the service they deserve!"

# How to Order Additional Books

To order more copies of Susan's book, simply photocopy this form, fill it out as shown, and return it to us at the address below. Checks or corporate purchase orders are preferred.

Or, visit us at www.servesyouright.net and download the order form there. We'll speed your order to you promptly!

Ask us about volume discounts for group trainings.

## Ordering Information for . . .

## SERVES YOU RIGHT!

*The Ins...the Outs...Great Customer Service*

_____ Paperback copies @ $15.95  =  $_____

7.7% sales tax (AZ residents only)  =  $_____

(allow 2-3 weeks) S&H @ $3 per book  =  $_____

Grand Total  =  $_____

Make checks payable to Serves You Right! Ink and mail to:
Serves You Right! Ink
6105 E. Osborn Road, Scottsdale, AZ 85251

☐ Check here if you want information about Susan Brooks trainings, workshops and motivational presentations. Her topics include:
- Service Enthusiasm®
- Service Enthusiasm® Boost!
- Serving the Inside Customer
- Stepping Up . . . Being Brave!
- The Entrepreneurial Spirit

NAME _____

COMPANY _____

ADDRESS _____

CITY _____ STATE _____ ZIP _____

☐ VISA   ☐ MASTERCARD                 EXPIRES _____

CREDIT CARD # _____

CARDHOLDER'S SIGNATURE _____

Serves You Right! Ink
(480) 994-1918 • Fax (480) 994-5966
www.servesyouright.net